EDUCATION
OF
EXCEPTIONAL CHILDREN

EDUCATION OF EXCEPTIONAL CHILDREN

Challenges and Strategies

Dr. PREM PRAKASH

M.A. (Psy., Eng.), M.Ed., Ph. D.

Principal

Greater Noida College of Education

Greater Noida

Distt. Gautam Buddh Nagar (U.P.)

KANISHKA PUBLISHERS, DISTRIBUTORS

NEW DELHI-110 002

KANISHKA PUBLISHERS, DISTRIBUTORS
4697/5-21A, Ansari Road, Daryaganj
New Delhi -110 002
Phones : 2327 0497, 232 8 8285
Fax : 011-2328 8285
E-mail : kanishka_publishing@yahoo.co.in
kanishkabooks@gmail.com

Education of Exceptional Children: Challenges and Strategies

First Published-2008

Edition-2023

ISBN : 978-81-8457-074-8

PRINTED IN INDIA

Published by Madan Sachdeva for Kanishka Publishers, Distributors, 4697/5-21A, Ansari Road, Daryaganj, New Delhi-110002, Typeset by Sunshine Graphics, Delhi, and Printed at G.S. Printers, Delhi.

In Loving Memory of
My Revered Mother
(The Fountain of Inspiration)

Preface

Full many a gem of purest ray serene,

The dark unfathom'd caves of ocean bear;

Full many a flower is born to blush unseen,

And waste its sweetness in the desert air.

THOMAS GRAY

The above quoted lines, composed by Thomas Gray are remarkable and aptly applicable truly depict to what extent our exceptional children' talent/creativity may go waste if we are unable to provide them proper and congenial educational environment at the proper time. The most significant factor to be stressed is the identification of their creative talent as early as possible so that their creative talent may blossom before it takes ill direction and wrong doings.

As psychologists and educationists discover more about the problems of exceptional learners' behaviour, our work becomes more and more pertinent to the solution of those poblems. This filed of psychology is now more concerned than ever before with the applications of psychological knowledge to solve problems of exceptional learners who are unable to benefit and gain the knowledge from the normal methods and techniques of teaching-learning process.

In planning this book, author has tried to capture the essence of exceptional learners and has presented it in a way that shows its diversity and complexity while striving to retain the readability and high interest level of the readers. All the chapters have been dealt in a very cogent and lucid manner. Language used is very simple and easy to be understood. It has also been kept in mind that the book may prove trustworthy, friend, philosopher and guide to all those who are interested in acquainting themselves adequately and educating exceptional learners. The exhaustive material will help to actualize and visualize the problems of exceptional children.

Author incorporated the following framework for unification of exceptional learners:

Flexibility uniqueness: It concerns the visually handicapped, deaf and hard of hearing, orthopaedically and other health impaired children.

Social uniqueness: It refers to emotionally disturbed, speech impaired, eating disorders, antisocial personality, behaviour problems and disadvantaged children.

Intellectually uniquencess: It focuses on the learning disabled, mentally retarded, gifted and backward children.

Special and Integrated Education

The author extends his grateful thanks to all other author and publishers whose books he had studied and quoted in the preparation of this volume. Suggestions for further improvement of the book will be highly appreciated. In the last of each chapter, the names of a few books have been suggested for further readings. Questions (long answer, short answer and objective type) have also been provided.

I shall be failing in my duty if I do not pay off debt of gratitude to Shri Madan Sachdeva of Kanishka Publishers and Distributors who has taken been interest in the publication of this book.

Best and warm wishes to the readers .

DR. PREM PRAKASH

Contents

1
Exceptional Children

No two individuals are alike and they are different in every aspect. In other words it may be stated that children are unique. If we observe their activities, we find that some are very quick in play activities, movements and have better flexibility and co-ordination than others. Some children are surrounded by admiring friends as they have the quality of leadership whereas others sit alone at some distance. The differences that are observed on the playground are more obvious than those who are inside the classrooms.

The term 'exceptional children', refers to children whose needs are very different from those of the majority of children in society and also refers to those who deviate from normal children in any way. These children are sufficiently below or above the average range. Certainly they need specialised attention which may not be provided in regular classrooms. It is obvious that educational objectives are similar to that of all other children of the school. The only difference lies in the means of education.

Definitions of Exceptional Children

According to Barbe, 'exceptional refers to those children who differ from the average to an extent that their differences warrant some type of special school adjustment either within the regular class-room or in special classes.'

In the words of Crow and Crow, 'the term typical or exceptional is applied to a trait or to a person possessing the trait if the extent of deviation from normal possession of that trait is so great that because of it, the individual warrants and receives special attention from the behaviour, responses and activities are thereby affected.'

Kirk defined, 'an exceptional child is he who deviates from the normal or average child in mental, physical and social characteristics to such an extent that he requires a modification of school practices or special educational services or supplementary instruction in order to develop to his maximum capacity.'

The above mentioned definitions explain the concept of exceptional children but it is also to be kept in mind that the difference is only in degree and they are more like other children than unlike them. "An exceptional learner is an individual who, because of uniqueness in sensory, physical, neurological, temperamental or intellectual capacity and/or in the nature or range of previous experience requires adoptions of the regular school programme in order to maximize his/her functioning level" (Hewett and Forness).

Most of the psychologists like Kirk in the field of special education have chosen to define exceptional children in the following way:

Dunn (1973)

'An exceptional pupil is so labelled only for that segment of his school career: *(i)* when his deviating physical or behavioural characteristics are of such a nature as to manifest a significant learning asset or disability for special education purposes and therefore *(ii)* when through trial provision, it has been determined that he can make greater all round adjustment and scholastic progress with direct or indirect special educational services than he could with only a typical regular school programme.'

Gear Heart (1972)

'The exceptional child shall be considered to be one whose educational requirements are so different from the average or normal child, that he cannot be effectively educated without the provision of special educational programmes, service facilities or materials.'

Most of the above mentioned definitions focused on attributes, deficiencies, defects of the child or important characteristics of those to whom special and professional attention is required. We may state that special education and exceptional children are synonymous and we should stress on their education which may be based on their psychological, sociological, emotional and physical needs. Thus we can explain that special education is that profession which is concerned with the arrangement and organization of educational variables leading to the prevention, reduction or elimination of those conditions that produce and reflect significant defects in the academic, communicative, locomotive or adjustive, functioning of children. In view of it, it may be stated that special education is an emerging applied science to plan, organize, control, design and deliver intervention with the object, purpose or goal for normalized development of all such children.

The committee for the National Society for the study of Education has described exceptional children as 'those who deviate from what is supposed to be average in physical, mental, emotional, social characteristics to such an extent that they require educational services in order to develop their maximum capacity.'

H.J. Baker stressed that these children do not form a separate class even they are not also distinct from normal children. Such devoted children require specialized attention which is not sufficient and satisfactorily provided in regular classrooms as these children are designated 'exceptional children'.

F.M. Hewett, and S.R., Forness, indicated the kinds of uniqueness that matter. They explained the field of special education is concerned with children who are unique in ways that matter when it comes to learning in school and functioning successfully elsewhere. This uniqueness is considered of as falling along a series of dimensions as shown in Table 1.1.

Identification of Uniqueness

The placement of an individual along the dimension of intelligence relied more on the use of an I.Q. test. For both dimensions of intelligence and the other six we believe on informal and formal observation.

Informal Observation

Parents of the child observe as he grows and matures. Some severe problems may be observable at birth whereas others may not become apparent until a later time. Visual or movement may be more readily identified at an earlier than a problem of hearing. Hearing problems become noticeable when child begins to speak in second or third years of life. At this juncture not only parents are engaged in on going informal observations but also relatives, friends and neighbours. Throughout early life and into the school years, parents, teachers and others who informally observe how children are functioning along the seven dimensions of exceptional learners.

Formal Observation

Factors Responsible for Differences Among Exceptional Learners

This kind of observation is generally or usually conducted by physician or other specialists trained to know-how children should function along the seven dimensions. Even though teachers can administer individual and group tests to obtain a more formal picture of child's functioning in academic field. Psychologist parents and teachers can formally observe children's behaviour by keeping their records of the kinds of problem of behaviour.

We now come to this conclusion that all individuals are learners. However, there are factors which are responsible for differences among exceptional learners. These factors are described as follow:

1. Capacity
2. Range and nature of experience
3. Functioning level.

1. *Capacity:* There are certain inherited characteristics or capacities for receiving and perceiving sensory stimuli and eliciting motor and verbal responses are fixed at birth. However certain limits are established by birth but experience plays a major role in determining whether our capacities are maximized or minimized.
2. *Range and Nature of Experience:* The range and nature of our experience make out visual stimuli and hear sounds. This range of experiences makes up our life time is underway. The range of experience from birth onward is important and critical in determining the level of functioning we attain. Children who born with a handicapped condition may suffer in terms of both the range and nature of experience. Over protection of the parents may lead to a narrow range of experience and their rejection may cause anxiety and unpleasantness to the child.
3. *Functioning Level:* Behaviour of the child is the result of complex interaction of capacity, the range and nature of experience. It may be called each child's functioning level. There are children whose capacity factor may primarily determine the behaviour of children in school, there are other children whose limited range of experience (deprived environment) may be primarily important. On some children rich experiences may have had the greatest effect on their functioning level. Whatever, the

reasons may be of behaviour of the children, reflects the interaction of both. Teachers can do nothing about capacity or the range and nature of previous experience but we have to accept the child's present level of functioning and do a great deal about their experiences and nature of future experiences. This is actually teaching-learning process which is the responsibility of the teacher to get it modified.

The Hewett and Forness are of the opinion that uniqueness rather than limitations, allows us to include the gifted learner in their definition.

This uniqueness within a framework suggested by Simpson, according to him human being is unique because of four interrelated concepts.

1. Flexibility,
2. Sociality (Socialization),
3. Intelligence, and
4. Individualization.

1. *Flexibility*

This concept include the dimensions as previously stated in Table 1.1 *i.e.*, visual, hearing, movement and perceptual motor.

2. *Sociality (Socialization)*

It refers to the unique human attributes of needing and interacting with each other. It includes the communication and social emotional dimensions as indicated earlier. We can state them as follows:

(*a*) Communicating effectively with others.
(*b*) Seeking social interactions.
(*c*) Establishing harmonious relationship with others.

3. *Intelligence*

The dimensions of intelligence with the uniqueness of exceptional learner include gifted and mentally retarded. However, we can judge them with the help of the followings:

(*a*) Competence in learning new things.
(*b*) The grasping of broad and subtle facts especially abstract facts.
(*c*) Ability to see relationship and plan for the future.
(*d*) Memory and the ability of profit from past experience.
(*e*) Ability to use symbols particularly verbal symbols.

4. *Individualization*

This unique attribute refers for human beings to achieve an almost unlimited variation in their growth and development and to career and vocational goals. This attribute relates to the outcome of an individual's development along all seven of the dimensions, discussed previously.

Now we are able to attempt to select the particular concept that appears most effective and relevant to the uniqueness of each type of exceptional learners.

1. *Flexibility Uniqueness*
   (*a*) Visually handicapped individuals.
   (*b*) Deaf and hard of hearing individuals.
   (*c*) Deaf blind individuals.
   (*d*) Orthopaedically and other health impaired individuals.
2. *Social Uniqueness*
   (*a*) Emotionally disturbed individuals.
   (*b*) Speech impaired individuals.
   (*c*) Emotionally disadvantaged and/or culturally disadvantaged individuals.
3. *Intellectual Uniqueness*
   (*a*) Individual with learning disabilities.
   (*b*) Mentally retarded individuals.
   (*c*) Gifted individuals.

Classifications/Categories of Exceptional Children

We can categories exceptional children in the following way:

1. Mental Retardation
2. Behaviour Disorders
   - Emotional Disorder
   - Social Maladjustment
3. Communicative Disorder
   - Stuttering
   - Language
     - Development delays
     - Aphasics

4. Physical Disabilities
    - Locomotion
    - Muscular Dysfunctioning
    - Motor Dysfunctioning

5. Learning Disabilities (Academics)
    - Reading
    - Writing
    - Arithmetic

6. Giftedness and creativeness.

Another kind of classification of exceptional children is given below:

1. Handicapped Children (Physically)

    (a) Visually handicapped children

    (b) Aurally handicapped children
    - *(i)* Conductive hearing loss
    - *(ii)* Sensory neural hearing loss
    - *(iii)* Psychogenic hearing loss
    - *(iv)* Central auditory defects

    (c) Speech handicapped children
    - *(i)* Disorder of articulation
    - *(ii)* Voice disorder (phonation)
    - *(iii)* Delayed speech
    - *(iv)* Stuttering and stammering

2. Mentally retarded children
3. Gifted children
4. Slow learner
5. Socially disadvantage children
6. Juvenilia delinquents
7. Backward children
8. Creative children.

Who are Exceptional Learners?

Hewatt, F.M. with Forness, S.R. in his book *Education of Exceptional Learners* classified exceptional learners in the following way:

Table–1.1
Dimensions of Exceptional Learners

Exceptional Learner	*Primary Dimensions (S)*	*Possible Related Dimensions*
1. Visually handicapped	Vision	Hearing, movement perceptual, motor, communication, social emotional
2. Deaf and Hard of hearing	Hearing	Vision and all above
3. Orthopaedically and other health impaired	Movement	Perceptual, motor, communication social, emotional, intelligence
4. Emotionally disturbed	Social emotional	Movement, perceptual, motor, communication
5. Speech impaired	Communication	Social-emotional
6. Disadvantaged	None	Vision, hearing, movement perceptual motor communication, social emotional
7. Learning disabled	Perceptual Motor communication	Movement, social, emotional
8. Mentally retarded	Intelligence	Vision, hearing and all dimensions
9. Gifted	Intelligence	Vision, hearing and all dimensions

Here it is to be noted that the related dimensions for the mentally retarded and the gifted are identical but each would fall in a normal curve in an opposite range on each dimension. There are seven critical dimensions related to successful learning in school and successful adaptations elsewhere. Hewett and Forness state, 'we all vary on each dimension but as we vary to a degree that adaptation of the regular school programme becomes necessary as does special consideration elsewhere, we become exceptional.'

1. Visually Handicapped

Visually handicapped children suffer from the impairment and defects of their eyes to such a degree as to make them full disabled or handicapped in terms of their visual ability and visual perception. Visual impairment restricts a child's learning environment. Totally visually impaired children (blind) face more difficulty than partially sighted for learning about size, colour, weight and emotional expressions. When we get to the point where a stimulus a person with normal vision can perceive at two hundred feet must be brought to within twenty feet. Before we can see it, we are legally blind and close to the extreme end of the visual deficit range. Visually handicapped individuals fall at varying points within this range and special education adapts the educational programme to compensate for their deficit. There are two broad categories named below:

(a) Totally blind children
(b) Partially blind children.

2. *Deaf and Hard of Hearing Children (Hearing Impaired Children)*

This dimension is very critical to learning, as the development of language is hearing. When children are unable to detect useful sounds, they fall far down the problem range and rely on lip-reading, signing and other methods for communication. Some severely handicapped individuals have extreme problems on both the dimensions of vision and hearing and is called deaf blind. In terms of physiological and medical language the hearing losses are generally classified into the following categories:

(a) Conductive Hearing Losses are caused by diseases in the outer or middle ear.
(b) *Sensory Neural Hearing Losses*: Such losses result from damage to the delicate sensory ear cells of the inner ear. These losses can range from mild to profound.
(c) *Psychogenic Hearing Losses*: The cause of such losses is purely psychological under a stressful situation, the child may unconsciously develop hearing loss as an escape from an intolerable situation.
(d) *Central Auditory Defects*: Children having such defects seem to be aware of sound but are unable to get its meaning.

3. *Orthopaedically and Other Health Impaired*

This is a movement dimension which is critical to individuals who are orthopaedically impaired and chronically ill. As movement due to crippling condition such as cerebral palsy limits them, they may need braces or a wheel chair.

4. *Emotionally Disturbed*

It is a dimension which is vague and more difficult to define than the other dimensions. Emotional disturbance is not quantifiable, as are blindness and deafness. Some children display problem behaviour in some situations and not in others such a problem behaviour is called disturbed by one individual might be called assertive or independent by another. The autistic child occupies the most extreme position in the problem range along this dimension.

5. Speech Impaired (Communication)

The communication dimensions are important and significant for many exceptional learners. Some of the individuals have difficulty making themselves understood. This involves a slight stutter, articulation problem or muteness at the extreme position in the problem range.

6. Learning Disabled (Perceptual Motor)

The perceptual motor dimension is concerned with how effectively and accurately children see and hear stimuli present in the environment. There are some children who perceive the word 'girl' and write as gril and the two spoken words perceive as identical. This is a problem for individuals with learning disabilities.

7. Gifted and Mentally Retarded (Intelligence)

Children who lack normal intelligence and those who have a superior intellect are all considered exceptional learners. Thus both positive and negative ranges of normal curve are concern to the field of special education.

8. Disadvantaged Children

Although there is no one primary dimension but have related possible, dimensions as indicated in Table 1.1. However, poverty is one of the oldest and wide spread of all handicapped conditions. It has also been constituted more of a problem for certain racial caste and ethnic groups than for others that is why we are supposed to discuss economically disadvantaged and/or culturally disadvantaged children.

All the above mentioned categories of exceptional learners shall be dealt chapter-wise in detail separately.

Needs of Exceptional Learners/ Children

We can classify needs of exceptional children in the following categories:

1. Academic needs of exceptional learners
2. Psycho-social needs of exceptional children.

Academic Needs of Exceptional Learners

1. *The Need of the Resource Teacher*

A resource teacher is a teacher who has specially been trained to assess to teach, to motivate by providing right incentives at the right time and evaluate the performance of the children identified as being in need of special educational services. He is also expected to work closely with the child's regular class teacher and his/her parents in order to provide the child with a consistent and integrated programme.

2. *Role of the Resource Teacher*

Resource teacher must be aware of the psycho-social needs of normal children; the some needs are also lying among the exceptional children. He should specifically tackle these students accordingly. A few psycho-social needs are being briefly described here for his knowledge, understanding and application.

Incentive

Resource teacher should describe some goal/object that may motivate their behaviour of exceptional learners. He should know that incentive differ in value for them from moment to moment in fact and from one time to another. Incentives are not innate but are learned. Thoughts can serve as incentive motivators. Incentives act as energizers. He should keep in mind while teaching them that different amounts or sizes of reward influence the rate of learning. Incentive motivation mediates between stimulus and response by creating emotional states as it is closely related and tied to the learning of emotional responses. Teacher, counsellor or resource person should know that hedonism approach acts as a motivator for such children too which can be defined as the seeking of pleasure and avoidance of pain.

Love or Belongingness Needs

These needs involve a hunger for affectionate relationships with others, a need to feel part of a group, or a feeling that 'one belongs'. Thwarting of these needs leads to behavioural maladjustment and pathology and it is the most common basis for behavioural problems for these exceptional children. Teacher or resource person should provide such an environment in the school where these needs may be fulfilled. Parents also think the psychological way of satisfying these needs in the home.

Esteem Need

The need for self-esteem motivates the individual to strive for achievement, strength, confidence, independence and freedom. The related need of esteem from others involves a desire for reputation, status, recognition, appreciation by others of one's abilities and a feeling of importance. No opportunity should be missed for them. Teacher must organize such activities where exceptional children may take part according to their physical and mental ability.

Level of Aspiration

The teacher or resource person must understand the level of past performance before fixing their level of future performance. Level of aspiration should be increased according to their success in the task.

Ego-involvement Learning

The ego-consists of attitude related to the self-respect. It is the teacher or resource teacher who should motivate exception children according to their ability and capacity by maximizing the involvement of ego in teaching-learning process.

Competition and Co-operation

Undoubtedly by competition is a source of motivation. It indicates the desire to excel others and develop level of achievement motivation (N-ach). However competition must be healthy which energize, their teaching-learning process in the right direction and create an atmosphere of co-operation among their peer groups.

Reward and Punishment

It is equal to praise and reproof. Both are powerful incentives and be may be used as the teaching-learning situation demands. These should be used psychologically and cautiously.

Effective Methods

Proper methods, strategies, aids and devices in teaching should be used according to their level of ability and needs which may be able to motivate them for learning.

There are other psycho-social needs which are to be satisfied in the school and home such as:

- *(i)* Need achievement (n-ach)
- *(ii)* Need affiliation (n-aff)
- *(iii)* Need power (n-pow).

2. *Trained Professional Personnel*

Teachers resource leaders educators, teachers, administrators, consultants all should be trained and should be specialized in the field of psychology of motivation.

3. *Course of Study*

Special course of study having content suiting to the exceptional learners should be prepared by the experts.

4. *Special Facilities*

Special facilities should be provided such as equipments, material and other infrastructure in view of their exceptionality. Besides motivating the exceptional learners followings are other functions of the resource teacher.

The Resource Teacher (RT) is to assist:

(i) The school administration in the identification and placement of these children.

(ii) RT has to organize in service orientation programmes for the teachers who are teaching in ordinary schools.

(iii) She/he is to provide expert advise to the 'class' teachers, who are teaching the children with special needs.

(iv) He/she has to provide regular classroom teachers the new informations so that they execute in the class especially for those children who need special education.

Need for Special Education to Exceptional Learners

The differences among children are found to the extent that it becomes essential to keep them in the range of exceptional children and it is realized that these children cannot be reached by normal educational methods and systems. The need for special education and training emerges. Therefore, it becomes necessary to provide different kinds of education and treatment to these exceptional learners, so that they can develop their abilities and capacities in special fields according to their potentialities.

Objectives of Special Education

1. The goal of special education to reach of maximum level of effectiveness in total subjects.
2. Both physical and mental conditions of the handicapped children are to be kept in mind.
3. Preparation of curriculum material that determine effective

and sound development of the personality of the particular typed handicapped children.

4. Proper and effective methods of incentive as already discussed above should be provided by the teachers, resource teachers as well as counsellors so that performance in learning may be maximized.
5. Inculcate interest among the handicapped children to participate in the co-curricular and extra-curricular activities (depend upon the handicappedness of the child).
6. Stress to develop realistic self-concept.

Educational Psychologist have formulated a set of axioms on which the special education stands which can be enumerated as follows:

1. Every child is unique and each exceptional learner is a child so he has to same right to get the same educational privileges.
2. Researches reveal the fact that there are wide individual differences among children in each domain of exceptionality.
3. Screening, identification and placement in special educational programmes are essential because exceptional children make optimal progress in educational institutions.
4. A special curriculum should be prepared to match the needs of the exceptional children.
5. The domain of exceptionality will determine the nature of material required.
6. Education for exceptional children should form an integral part of the total educational programmes.
7. Continuous re-assessment process of exceptional children is essential.
8. There should be placement assistance for each student.
9. Exceptional children need special learning methods, special syllabi and special teachers. If they are not paid proper attention they become problem children and harm themselves and also the society. So special education for them becomes the special need.
10. To provide understanding the problems of exceptional children, special education helps to parents and teachers in this regard.
11. The needs of exceptional are so different from normal children that it becomes the responsibility of the Government to make arrangements to provide them rightful education.

QUESTIONS

A. Long Answer Type Questions

1. Discuss the concept of 'exceptional children'? How will you arrange their education?
2. Define 'exceptional children' Discuss its different types.
3. Discuss the psychological needs of exceptional children. Are these needs are important? Why?
4. Discuss need and objectives of special education for exceptional children.

B. Short Answer Type Questions

1. Define and explain the definition of exceptional children given by Barke.
2. Special education for exceptional children is essential, Why? Discuss.
3. Who is handicapped child?
4. Who needs special education?

C. Objective Type Questions

1. Who can be considered as psychologically handicapped children:
   (*a*) Emotionally unstable (*b*) Disadvantaged
   (*c*) Orthopaedically handicapped (*d*) Learning disabled
2. Residential schools for exceptional children are based on the technique:
   (*a*) Segregation (*b*) Interaction
   (*c*) Mutual understanding (*d*) Co-operation
3. Special schools are essentially not needed of which class of handicapped.
   (*a*) Mentally retarded (*b*) Creative
   (*c*) Orthopaedically handicapped (*d*) Co-operation

SUGGESTIVE READINGS

1. Backer, H.J. (1956). *Introduction to Exceptional Children,* Boston Sergeant.
2. Heck, A.O. (1940). *Education of Exceptional Children,* New York, Mc Graw Hall.
3. Skinner, C.E. (1968). *Educational Psychology* (4th Ed), New Delhi, Prentice Hall of India.
4. Shanker, U. (1976). *Exceptional Children,* New Delhi, Sterling Publishers.
5. Telford, C.N. and Sawrey, J.M., (1967), *The Exceptional Individual* New Jersey, Prentice Hall Inc.

2

Visually Handicapped Individuals

The visually handicapped individual's condition evokes marked most emotional response as compared to other handicapped conditions. The visually handicapped child who is born blind or whose vision was lost during the early years must rely on the remaining senses of hearing, touch, and to a lesser extent taste and small for knowledge of the environment and for clues for successful adoption. However, blindness is not always total. Thus almost 60 per cent of the estimated blind had enough vision to distinguish between light and dark and to see the moving hand at a distance of one foot. They are diagnosed as blind because they had less than 20/200 vision in the better eye after correction and/or because they were severely handicapped by a restricted visual field.

Definitions of Visual Impairment

The term 'visual impairment' is used to refer to not only those who are blind, but also those who have low vision.

According to Legal Definition of Blindness

If a person's visual acuity is 20/200 or less in the better eye, even after the best possible correction with eye glasses or contact lenses, then he is considered to be blind. A person may also be considered legally blind, if his field of vision is extremely restricted. The field of vision is the total area in which perception is possible when the individual is looking straight ahead.

'Visually handicapped' means a visual impairment which, even with correction, adversely affects a child's educational performance. The term includes both partially seeing and blind children.

Scholl (1975) found several limitations in these legal definitions of visual impairment concern the special educator. According to the American Academy of Ophthalmology and International Council of Ophthalmology, it is useful to classify visual handicaps in terms of visual performance (Freeman, and Scott, 1977). It has been proposed that visually impaired individuals be grouped functionally as follows:

1. Normal or near-normal vision indicates the ability to perform all visual tasks adequately with special aids.
2. Low vision indicates that without special aids, a person is unable to perform tasks that normally required detailed vision.
3. Blindness means that, without increased reliance on other senses, a person is unable to perform tasks that normally require gross vision.

Berthold Lownfeld presents a moderate position of blind. He says that blindness imposes three basic limitations on the individual.

1. In the range and variety of experiences.
2. In the ability to get about.
3. In the control of the environment and the self in relation to it.

These three restrictions Lownfeld views as 'the objective effects of blindness.' The clinical measurement must fall within the specific parameters which were adopted by the American Medical Association (AMA). 'Central visual acquity of 20/200 or less in the better eye with corrective glasses of central visual acquity of more than 20/200 if there is a visual field defect in which the peripheral field is contracted to such an extent that the wider diameter of the visual field subtends an angular distance no greater than 20 degrees in the better eye (Kestler, 1976).

Classifications of Visual Impairment

Visually handicapped are classified in the following categories in view of educational purpose.

1. *Blind:* The person who learns through tactile or auditory materials (Caton, 1981).
2. *Low Vision:* Severely visually impaired are those who after correction can increase visual function (Corn, 1980).

3. *Limited Vision:* Persons who can use their vision limited under average circumstances (Barraga, 1983).

According to World Health Organization (WHO)

1. *Low Vision*
   (a) Severe performs visual tasks at a reduced level.
   (b) Profound difficulty with gross visual tasks.
2. *Blind*
   (a) Near blind (vision unreliable)
   (b) Blind (totally without sight)

Identification and Diagnosis

The National Society for the Prevention of Blindness (1965) considers the following ten behavioural signs as possible indicators of visual defects.

1. Attempting to brush away blurs, rubbing eyes excessively, frowning.
2. Shutting or covering one eye, tilting head or thrusting it forward when looking at near or distant objects.
3. Difficulty in reading or in other work requiring close use of eyes.
4. Blinking more than usual, crying often, irritability when doing close work.
5. Stumbling or tripping over small objects.
6. Holding books or small objects close to eyes.
7. Inability to participate in games requiring distance vision.
8. Excessive sensitivity to light.
9. Red-rimmed, encrusted or swollen eyelids, recurring sites, inflamed or watery eyes, crossed eyes.
10. Complaints of not seeing well, of dizziness, headaches or nausea following close eye work of blurred or double vision.

Growth and Development of Visually Impaired Children

It is very essential and significant to understand the growth and development of children with visual impairments. Growth is defined typically as an increase in size and quantitative changes. Development is an increase of complexity, or qualitative change (Olison, 1959). The terms are usually used together since quantitative and qualitative changes are a clear distinction between them is often difficult to determine. The process of growth and development is at the same time is similar for all children and unique for each child

(Mussen, Conger and Kagan, 1979). This principle applies to children with visual impairments as well and in general growth and development tends to be more alike than different from that of handicapped children. Variation in their growth and development can usually be attributed to influence related to the visual impairment either directly or indirectly. Direct influences are those which result from the visual impairment, e.g. as restrictions in the acquisition of certain cognitive concepts that require the use of vision, such as colour or three dimensions. In direct influences are those found in the ecology or environment in which the child lives which can restrict and deprive him of opportunities and experiences because of attitudinal factors and lack of knowledge about the nature of the visual impairment. Both type of influences are interrelated and exert a mutual influence upon each other.

Characteristics of the Visual Impairment

Children who lose their vision before the age of five years are usually considered as congenitally visually handicapped for educational purposes because they retain relatively little visual imagery and memory for colour (Lowenfeld, 1980).

Children who lose their vision after the age of five years may have greater difficulty becoming tattle rather than visual learners and may also evidence accompanying emotional reactions to their loss of vision particularly when the loss occurs as late as adolescence (Lowenfeld, 1980). Teachers and parents must be sensitive to potential educational and emotional effects. Thus, it is important to know the diagnosis of the child's visual impairment and its potential accompanying impact on behaviour and learning.

Parents, teachers and community tend to expect more from children who have partial vision, thus placing more stress and pressure on them to perform as a person with normal vision. The child with limited vision may view himself as belonging to neither the sighted nor the visually handicapped world which may result in a reduced self-concept or emotional problems. Prognosis, the future of eye condition, frequently has implications. Parents and teachers need to be aware and potentially deteriorating vision in order to help the child adjust to and prepare for the eventual visual loss adolescents may need to consider this possibility in their planning.

Variations in Children with Visual Impairments (Motor Development)

Child with visual impairment during the first few months of life is not markedly different than that of the non-handicapped child (Warren, 1984). In later motor development, there are indirect influences which can and often do have an impact on the process, however the visual impairment does not retard physical and motor development but rather are related to the factors such as:

- *(i)* Characteristics of visual impairment,
- *(ii)* Lack of visual stimulation,
- *(iii)* Lack of vicarious learning, and
- *(iv)* Environmental factors.

(i) Characteristics of Visual Impairment

The etiology of the visual impairment may also cause other disabilities which can retard physical and motor development such as brain damage, severe mental retardation and cerebral palsy.

(ii) Lack of Visual Stimulation

Lack of vision deprives the infant to an appreciation that leads to an appreciation of the role that vision plays in stimulating psycho-motor development as early visual tracking motivates the infant to reach and grasp.

(iii) Lack of Vicarious Learning

Much of early learning takes place through imitation, primarily visual imitation (Miller, 1983). The child with any degree of visual impairment has a more limited access to this way or mode of learning.

(iv) Environmental Factors

Many children with visual impairments are retarded in their physical growth and development because the environmental factors particularly the early environment of the home. Parents may over protect and fail the provide opportunities to learn.

The role of the parents and teachers in the developmental process is critical. Early intervention is essential if the child is to develop normally. The opportunities to satisfy basic needs for movement and activity must be provided from earliest infancy otherwise the child with a severe impairment will seek to satisfy the need within himself rather than outside himself and gain his satisfaction from seemingly aimless physical activities or stereotypic behaviours, sometimes referred to as 'blindisms'.

Cognitive Development Variations in Children with Visual Impairments

A visual impairment places a child at a disadvantage of cognitive development specially in the area of *(i)* sensory stimulation, *(ii)* concept development, and *(iii)* communication (Lowenfeld, 1981). Lowenfeld lists three restrictions of blindness on the cognitive development.

1. On the range and variety of experiences,
2. On the ability to move about, and
3. On the control of the environment.

The child is deprived of a valuable source of sensory input with the result that development may take place more slowly and be uneven across specific intellectual abilities. A rich background of experience will help the child with a visual impairment to achieve more cognitive development. The programmes for parents and early childhood education are essential in order to reduce the disadvantages imposed by the visual impairment. Many concrete experiences are needed especially during the sensory motor stage to enable the child to develop knowledge about the object world. Other resources of sensory input must be exploited to the maximum.

Affective Development Variation in Children with Visual Impairment

It is difficult to separate cognitive from affective development since they are interrelated and exert mutual influences on each other (Joffee Vaughn, 1982). The visual impairment has little direct influence on affective development but indirect influences can exert a significant impact. The lack of early eye contact can retard the bonding that is necessary between mother and infant (Frailberg *et al.*, 1963). Some parents may react negatively to the lack of eye contact, thereby setting up a cycle of reinforcement that retards the development of an adequate and meaningful relationship between parent and child. The more of the child from family into peer groups may be hundred because the child cannot see to imitate his/her peers or to utilize non-verbal communication skills in order to know when he is acceptable, if he is not acceptable, he cannot initiate the necessary behaviours to secure acceptance.

Adolescence may be a particularly difficult time because any degree of visual impairment will set the child apart as they cannot see the latest fads in clothing, mannerisms, expressions and other aspects of adolescents life, girls in particular are at a disadvantage. Early intervention programmes are essential to assist parents in their adjustment to the advent of a visually handicapped into the family. The ultimate adjustment of the person with a visual handicap is dependent in large measure on the attitude of parents, their own adjustment and their adjustment to the child who is visually impaired. Thus, parents should be helped to develop positive attitude in this regard.

Causes of Visual Impairment

Visual impairment can come up while the baby is in the mother's womb, during the time when the baby is being born, or after birth. If the child is born with visual impairment then it is called congenital from the visual impairment. If the person becomes visually impaired after the time of birth, it is known as adventitious form of visual impairment. Some of the causes of visual impairment are discussed below:

1. *Pre-natal Causes (Before Birth)*
   - *(a)* History of visual impairment in the family.
   - *(b)* Consanguineous marriages (marriages between close relatives).
   - *(c)* Blood group complications.
   - *(d)* Infectious diseases specially syphilis and rubella. Rubella is known to have caused major increase in visual impairment. It is a virus disease that is often to difficult to diagnose. If the disease is contracted during the first three months of pregnancy or sometimes later, the virus may kill or cripple by crossing the placental barrier and attacking the foetus. The virus is capable of killing growing cells and attacks tissues of the eyes, ears and other organs. However, the development of vaccine (rubella) has led to a marked decrease in the occurrence of the disease in expectant mothers.
   - *(e)* Poor health of the pregnant mother.
   - *(f)* Intake of antibiotics which are not prescribed by a doctor.
   - *(g)* Exposure to X-rays during pregnancy.
   - *(h)* Malnutrition particularly vitamin 'A' deficiency.

2. *Perinatal Causes (During Birth)*
   (a) Premature delivery.
   (b) Low birth weight of the baby.
   (c) Lack of oxygen to the infant during delivery.
   (d) Delivery using instruments (such as forceps wrongly may cause damage to parts of the brain responsible for seeing).
3. *Post-natal Causes (After Birth)*
   (a) Infectious disease.
   (b) Injury to the eye.
   (c) Tumours of the eye.
   (d) Neglect infection of the eye.
   (e) Vitamin 'A' deficiency.

The above mentioned causes indicate that both heredity and environment can lead to visual impairment.

Social Problems of Visually Impaired Children

The social consequences of their uniqueness may have a greater impact on their lives than the physiological or flexibility problem itself *e.g.* people may not like to talk, they may move away or enter the room without being heard. The social world of the blind can be an uncertain and frustrating one.

Much of the disability of blind and visually impaired people is occasioned by restrictions, overprotection, rejection, unrealistic expectations and the ignorance of society. He is further handicapped by being excused from the usual developmental, educational and vocational experiences and often being permitted to maintain unpleasant habits, poor posture, and a debilitating dependence. The fear occasioned in others by blindness is associate not only with the rejection of blind persons, but also often with a confining benevolence which cares for but also segregates them from sighted society (Connor and Muldoon, 1973).

Rejection of blind children also may be associated with limited knowledge about the visually handicapped. Teachers and administrators selected the visually handicapped as the least preferred teaching (except aggressive delinquents) from among eight categories of exceptional children (Murphy, 1960).

Intellectual Characteristics of Visually Impaired Children

Visually impaired children do not differ markedly from children from normal vision in terms of intelligence (Hayes, 1941). However, they seem to be more limited than sighted individuals in learning abstract concepts. There is some indication that blind children retain experiences or facts and are able to conceptualize but do both in a more concrete and less integrated fashion than do sighted children (Lowenfeld, 1980). It has also been reported that seeing children show significantly higher imagination in play, spontaneous fantasy, and dreams, whereas visually handicapped demonstrate more concreteness and lack of flexibility (Singer and Steiner, 1966).

Educational Provision and Treatment

Any child consistently manifesting one or more rights as indicated earlier should be referred to the school doctor for the intensive examination. The doctor can prescribe treatment including medication and glasses. The eyes of the school children should be routinely examined periodically thereafter for the discovery not only of errors of refraction and muscular defects but also of disorders developing from injuries or infections. The low vision may be assigned to sight saving glasses conducted in well-illuminated rooms (50 foot candles in all parts) free from outside or inside glare, equipped with non-glare movable furniture and special didactic materials such as books printed in large, clear 18 to 24 point type and cream coloured paper, and heavily leaded pencils. The pupils prepare their lesson in these classes and recite with pupils with normal vision. Assignments should be made to these classes only after competent ophthalmologist's examinations.

Blind children should be taught the reading and writing of Braille on the Braille state or typewriter in Braille classes in schools or in residential schools. When the Braille class is in the school, the pupils should be provided frequent contact with the seeing pupils in the regular classroom. A number of devices have been developed to the blind in reading. A recent developed technology resulted Optacon—a portable electronic device that include a camera for converting print to vibrating letter images. This is accomplished by a photo chemical to mechanical energy conversion process.

Both the partially sighted and the blind may be profit from a talking calculator. Once basic mathematical skills are mastered, the calculator can be used as any electronic calculator with the exception that numerical entries are read aloud to the students through an earplug. Tap recordings are very important tools for learning. Teachers of such children often serve as resource teachers in the school. They are available to work with students to help them acquire basic reading, mathematical, and written language skills by providing the necessary technical aids, Braille materials or equipments. Once the blind child is integrated into a regular school programme, the special education teacher serves as a tutor and resource teacher continuing basic skill development and aiding with home-work assignments on a scheduled basis.

Variety of Educational Options

The kinds of educational services are available for children with visual impairment are primarily the followings:

1. *Inclusive Education:* When the regular schools are equipped to meet the educational needs of the visually impaired children.
2. *Integrated Education:* When the regular schools are equipped with special teacher's assistance for children with visual impairment.
3. *Residential School:* Residential school facilities for visual impaired children are provided for those who do not have educational services near their homes. The residential school are also called special schools.
4. Home bound educational services are provided to those who have additional disabilities and who cannot attend any typed of schools.

Parents and teachers have an important role in helping the child to overcome limitations imposed due to visual impairment, by providing opportunities, stimulation, and encouragement for fostering development in different areas. Simultaneously the principal and teachers need to realize themselves that education is a right of children with disability. It is not as if the sighted are doing the visually impaired in favour by allowing them to get education. Only when the teachers of school themselves believe in this philosophy, will they be able to integrate a disabled child. Principals and teachers need to adopt the following strategies:

1. Need to overcome their own inhibitions and negative ideas.
2. Make the general classroom teachers aware of the needs, rights and capabilities of children with disability.

3. To organize advocacy and awareness programmes.
4. To organize parent-teacher association meetings.
5. To promote child-to-child learning for enriching educational experiences.

QUESTIONS

A. Long Answer Type Questions

1. Who are visually handicapped children? Discuss preventive measures to overcome their problems.
2. Discuss the educational provisions for partially sighted and blind children.
3. Define visual impairment. Discuss its various causes.
4. How can a visually impaired child be identified? Classify visual impairments.
5. How do growth and development affect on the behaviour of the visually impaired children? Discuss.

B. Short Answer Type Questions

1. Who is visually handicapped child? Discuss.
2. Classify visual impairment.
3. Variations in children with visual impairment especially on motor development.
4. Cognitive developmental variations with visual impaired children.
5. Causes of visual impairment .
6. Social problems of visually impaired children.
7. Intellectual characteristics of visually impaired children.
8. Discuss variety of education options.

C. Objective Type Questions

1. Consanguineous marriages is one of the causes of visual impairment. True/False
2. Rubella is caused major increase in visual impairment . True/False
3. The social consequences of visual impaired child have a greater impact on their lives as compared to physiologically impaired. True/False
4. Visual impairment may be due to:
   1. Premature delivery
   2. Lack of oxygen during delivery

   (*a*) 1 is true 2 is false (*b*) 2 is true 1 is false
   (*c*) both are false (*d*) both are true
5. 1. Deficiency of Vitamin 'B' is one of the causes of visual impairment

2. Deficiency of Vitamin 'A' is one of the causes of visual impairment.

(*a*) 1 is true 2 is false (*b*) 2 is true 1 is false

(*c*) both are true (*d*) both are false

SUGGESTED READINGS

1. Hewett, F.M. and Forness, S.R., (1984). *Education of Exceptional Learners* (3rd ed.), Allyn and Bacon. Inc. London.
2. Jones, R.L., *Attitudes and Attitude Change in Special Education: Theory and Practice.* Reston, Va Council for Exceptional Children.
3. Schulz, P. (1980). *How Does it Feel to be Blind?* Van Nuys, Calif, Muse—Ed.
4. Gardener, H. (1983). *Developmental Psychology: An Introduction* (2nd ed), Boston, Mass: Little, Brown and Company.
5. Lowenfeld, B. (1981). *Berthold and Lowenfeld on Blindness and Blind People,* New York, American Foundation for the Blind Inc.

3

Aurally Handicapped Children or Deaf and Hard of Hearing Individuals

Hearing of spoken language is one of the most important and significant experiences of developing human life. Language is related to hearing which plays a critical role in the socialization of the individual and in the educational process. It is the main sensory pathway through which speech, language, and verbal communication develop. If a child does not hear perfectly, it is likely to speak and think imperfectly and also influences perception, learning and other aspects of development of the child. Early detection of hearing impairment is important for the child's harmonious development as it reduces our knowledge of the world around us. It affects adversely too on the child's performance in learning. Educationally 'an aural handicap is such a disability which obstructs a child in taking an education by verbal expression.' Generally verbal expression has specific significant in teaching-learning process. Thus such a handicapped child require the help of special instruments and special education.

Meaning of Deafness

The term 'deaf' signifies that a person has minimal or no hearing. We use this term to denote any person whose auditory sense organ is damaged to the extent so as to preclude the auditory development and comprehension of speech or language with or without sound amplification.

The term 'deafness' means either partial or total loss of hearing. Hearing impairment and 'deafness' both imply a loss of sensitivity of hearing in the ear mechanism.

Definition of Deaf and Hard-of-Hearing

Hearing handicapped individuals are divided into two categories according to the law—1. The Deaf and 2. The Hard-of-Hearing.

1. *Deaf*

'Deaf' means a hearing impairment which is so severe that the child is impaired in processing linguistic information through hearing, with or without amplification, which adversely affects educational performance.

2. *Hard-of-Hearing*

It means a hearing impairment, whether permanent or fluctuating which also affects adversely a child's educational performance which is not included under the definition of 'deaf'.

The child who suffers a hearing loss after he/she developed speech and language is more fortunate than the child who is born deaf or with a hearing impairment. Generally the later, the hearing loss occurs, the less serious its effect on oral communication, since maintenance of speech and language is much less difficult than its acquisition (Avery, 1975).

Hearing is usually measured in terms of decibels (dB), a logarithmic unit of sound intensity above an arbitrary reference point. This reference point is established as the average level at which normal hearing adults, using both ears, can detect the faintest sound of which they are capable (Davis, 1970).

It may be defined, 'a deaf person cannot hear below 70dB of intensity and cannot understand speech by means of the ear alone or with the use of hearing aid.

The hard-of-hearing person requires 35 to 69 dB of intensity and although it may be difficult, to understand speech through the ear alone with or without a hearing aid.

Flexibility Characteristics of Impaired Hearing Individuals

The available data indicates that the visual system is less effective than the auditory system for receiving and comprehending spoken language. The effects of impaired hearing on flexibility become clearer when we consider the role of hearing in a child's exploration and adjustment in the environment. When deafness occurs, the individual loses the basic sense for environment contact and exploration and must use vision for both foreground and background. Scanning vision is not efficient monitoring sense for the environment because the individual must look up from and leave what he or she is doing and thinking in order to maintain an awareness of what is happening.

Social Characteristics of Hearing Impaired Individuals

The hearing handicapped individual is often at a serious disadvantage when interacting with others;

1. A loss of 30 to 45 dB makes conversation difficult without amplification. This level of hearing loss appears to affect basic awareness and monitoring rather than socialization.
2. A loss of 45 to 60 decibels clearly affects social interaction. There is a sense of detachment from others, and social relationships with those who have similar hearing problems may be preferred.
3. A loss of 70 decibels at this level amplification is less satisfactory for maintaining social relationships. Reliance on visual and actual senses becomes considerable.

Deafness is associated with a loss of 85 or more decibels.

The deaf are somewhat self-centred because they lack understanding of the emotions of others that are communicated by language (Sanders, 1980). Deafness itself does not cause emotional problems or mental illness. Social maturity of deaf children is concerned, it may be concluded that they are often less mature than are hearing children (Myklebust, 1964). This appear to be the result of the higher levels of social competence required with advancing years and deaf children's difficulty in attaining self-help and self-direction skills needed to meet these levels.

Intellectual Characteristics of Hearing Impaired Individuals

Hearing impaired children have problems in language development while intelligence is considered as the ability to learn, to adjust and to carry on abstract thinking. All considerations assume the presence of language and symbols language is learned relatively easily by hearing children from birth as they continually listen to people talk about surrounding environment and feeling at the moment those experiences happen with them. The child with hearing impairment cannot do like hearing child until his/her problem is detected and some measure initiated to compensate for it.

Research on deaf individuals seems to suggest that deaf children do not differ significantly from hearing children in their thinking process (Furth and Youniss, 1971). This conclusion supports Piaget's theory that language is not a basic element of logical thinking.

The effect of hearing handicaps on school learning becomes dramatically apparent in the area of academic achievement. On the average, deaf children are atleast three to four years below grade level and partially hearing children are from one half to two years behind (McConnell, 1973).

Behavioural Characteristics

Such children develop a sense of inferiority as they are helpless in adopting to circumstances that require verbal communication. The attitude of the society as the hearing impaired child observes, is not normal but it is overprotective, rejective or sympathetic which actually hampers growth and development of the personality. Hard of hearing child gets more frustration as he tries to reach the level of the normals. The young hearing impaired children show abnormal emotional behaviour. They may show tantrums to draw the attention to him or of their needs. They may develop obstinacy and the tendency to tease others. He gets irritated when he is unable to make himself understood.

Classification of Hearing Impairments

Some of the educationists have divided hearing impairment into two sub-groups.

1. *Pre-lingual Deaf:* Such a child is one who is born with little or no hearing. His/her impairment becomes apparent before speech and language patterns are acquired.
2. *Post-lingual Deaf:* Such a child is one who becomes a deaf due to environmental forces. His/her impairment becomes apparent after he has attained speech and language pattern.

All the hearing impairment persons can medically be classified into the following categories:

1. *Conductive Hearing Loss:* It is common among the hearing impairment of children. This results in the reduction in the loudness of the sound. The main cause may be the pathological changes in the middle ear due to congenital or acquired abnormalities of the ear.
2. *Sensory Neural Hearing Loss:* Abnormalities in the inner ear

or the auditory nerve result in loss of hearing. Hearing aids for amplification of sound has little to do with this defect. The sound is properly conducted and the difficulty lies in analysing or perceiving it properly. The therapy to remove this defect is purely educational.

3. *Psychogenic Hearing Loss:* The cause of this type/kind of the disorder is psychological. The child exaggerates symptoms of hearing impairment. The child may develop hearing loss as an escape from what to him is an intolerable situation. However, it is difficult to differentiate between organic defects and psychogenic losses. Only proper audiological techniques may help to find out the real etiology of the disorder.
4. *Central Auditory Defect:* This type of defect is extremely complex and its cause is poorly understood. Children who suffer from this defect are unable to discriminate its meaning. This causes severe communication problems. The percentage of this defect appears to be very high during early years of growth and development. Such children require extensive and prolonged individual thereby.

Table 3.1
Hearing Levels of Speech Perception in Decibels (dB)

Sl. No.	*Category*	*Level of Hearing Loss in Decibels*	*Education Placement*	*Special Aids*
1.	Normal	0-15 dB	Able to hear all sound including whispering	No
2.	Marginal near normal	16–30 dB	Unable to hear the whispering Required modification in seating arrangements in IED (Integrated Education for Disabled)	No
3.	Mild	31–45 dB	Unable to hear speech in public places	Hearing aid
4.	Moderate	46–60 dB	Loss to communicate by means of normal conversation	More visual cues
5.	Severe	61–90 dB	Unable to understand without proper amplification. Require special class	Use of special technique
6.	Profound	91dB and above	Even with amplification unable to use residual hearing for speech perception. Feels discomfort when amplified special day school	Intensive special instructor

Identification and Diagnosis

Teachers and parents play important and significant role in identifying hearing handicapped children. They may be requested to evaluate and locate some children who need help. Most of such children may not be identified because they hear conversational speech and learn to talk at an average age. A loss of thirty or forty decibels often is unnoticed and their deviant behaviour may be attributed to low intelligence or having emotional problems.

Group Screening test of all school children should be conducted periodically to identify hearing handicapped children. If any child who appears to have hearing-handicappedness, he should be individually examined and evaluated. Such a test should be conducted by an audiologist under the supervision of an otologist (a physician who can determine the exact nature of the hearing difficulty). The specialist is able to findout wax in the child's ear, infected adenoids or tonsils or some other abnormality that can be corrected. The audiologist and otologist can also recommend the type of hearing aid that may improve the child's learning.

Hearing impaired children may also be identified by taking into consideration their developmental status. In this regard 'Bayley Scales of Infant Development test is important to understand the child's sensorimotor development. This test will be very helpful for this purpose. If the sensorimotor development of the child is retarded, this scale will provide a basis for early diagnosis and corrective action. The case study method may also be adopted to identify the child's hearing impairment. This method helps teacher, clinical psychologist, psychiatrist to identify and recommend its remedy if possible.

The systematic observation of child's behaviour is important and significant to identify child's hearing impairment. The children generally display observable point of behaviour that indicate their hearing impairment. Some of the observable points of behaviour are:

1. Turning of head on one side to hear better.
2. Such hearing impaired children are unable to follow directions.
3. They always want and request to repeat instructions, questions etc.
4. The attention is focused on the speaker's lip.
5. They avoid to participating in group discussions.

6. They have poor communication skill.
7. They display restlessness and have speech difficulty.

Causes of Hearing Impairment

The most common identified causes of childhood deafness are: heredity, maternal rubella, meningiti and mother-child blood incompatibility (Moores, 1978).

Mother–child blood incompatibility occurs when the mother and foetus have different Rh blood group factors or when the mother has blood group O and the foetus has blood group A or B.

External and Middle Ear–Hearing Loss

1. *Impacted Wax:* Sometimes it happens that the wax may become hard in the canal and become impacted so that it prevents the sound waves from reaching the drum and the middle ear. A droplet of water may close the channel by way of creating hurdles from the effective reception of ordinary sounds.
2. *Congenital Malformations:* It is known as absence of the external hear or the pinna which may cause a mild loss of hearing.
3. *External Otitis:* It permits the growth of bacteria and fungi in the skin of external canal which produce a condition is called external otitis. It also causes hearing impairment.
4. *Otosclerosis:* It is a bone disease that affects the bony capsule surrounding the inner. The new bony growth fixes the stapes firmly in the oval window so that the stapes no longer moves freely and then the vibration carried to it from the drum head are not effectively transmitted to the fluid of the inner ear.

Other Abnormalities of the Middle Ear

Tumors, syphilis, tuberculosis, fracture of the skull and variety of other medical conditions may involve the ear that causes hearing impairments.

Inner Year Impairment

1. *Presbycusis:* It is a condition of inner ear hearing loss. It happens due to advancing of age.
2. *Drugs and Poisons:* The excessive use of certain drugs (like quinine and aspirin) may cause some sensory–neural hearing

loss if taken during pregnancy may affect the hearing of the foetus.

3. *Noise:* Sometimes noise may cause both temporary and permanent hearing impairment, as loud noise affects hearing.

Causes of Deafness After Birth

1. *Illness:* It is due to illness of the child. Measles, Smallpox, Chickenpox, Typhoid, Mum etc., are also the cause of deafness.
2. *Accidents:* Causing injuries in the internal ear membrane and the person suffers hearing impairment.
3. Psychological and emotional factors become the causes of hearing impairment.

Treatment and Educational Provisions to the Children Having Hearing Impairments

Teaching Language Skills to Deaf Children

A controversy has existed among those concerned with this skill. To what degree, if any manual communication be taught alongwith lip reading and speech?

Manual communication consists of both finger spelling and signing.

1. *Finger Spelling Means:* A series of twenty-six hand configurations representing the letters of the alphabets, a person who communicates through finger spelling holds his/her hand in front of the chest and spells each word, letter by letter, with hand configurating.
2. *Signing:* A second manual communication approach uses word signs instead of a literal letter-by-letter spelling of a word. Each sign has three elements:
   - *(a)* the position of the hands.
   - *(b)* the configuration of the hands.
   - *(c)* the movement of the hands to different positions.

There has been a controversy over the best method of teaching skills to hearing impaired children. The controversy is whether to include finger spelling and/or signing in the language training process.

Oralists prohibit gestures and signs and teach only lip-reading and speech. The Rochester method combines finger spelling and oral training whereas total communication method consists of oral training finger spelling and the use of signs. Thus method used most widely now-a-days. The following factors contribute to the increased use of this method (Total communication).

1. The recognition that a language of signs is a true language.
2. The recognition of purely manual or oral methods has limitations for the profoundly deaf.
3. The increasing militancy of deaf adults who had strict oral training but who have come to recognise the advantages of total communication.
4. The increased interest in sign language by hearing people.

Education for deaf children is provided in residential schools, day schools and special classes in public schools. Whether a deaf child should be placed in a day school or residential school programme? It cannot be made on the basis of which is most effective educational setting, but it should be considered what is most beneficial for a particular child in a particular community (Kirk, 1972).

If adequate resources are available at home, such children are probably best placed in a day school or class. Children having hearing impairment are at a serious disadvantage in learning to communicate and understand human language. Our primary concern should be plan treatment and educational programme for children who are deaf or partially hearing.

Hard-of-Hearing Children

Such children have adaptability of language hence they can be educated with hearing aids in the class of normal children. The following help may be given to them.

(i) Regular use of auditory aids.
(ii) Attempt to develop listening power.
(iii) Lip-reading.
(iv) Speech development—their speech may be modified slowly and slowly through special training. Such children learn by watching lip movements, facial expressions, signs and gestures. Parents should share the responsibility of their children for the successful integrations.

Teachers in the school should made efforts to extend all possible help and co-operation, so that hearing impaired children adjust themselves without having any difficulty. They should encourage, motivate and appreciate to such children to participate in the programmes wherever possible. Special programmes may be organized, especially for such children for their development.

QUESTIONS

A. Long Answer Type Questions

1. Who is aurally handicapped child? Discuss various causes of hearing impairments.
2. Discuss the problems of hearing impaired children. What type of treatment you would provide them.
3. Discuss the educational provisions for 'deaf' and 'hard-of-hearing' children.
4. Write a note on language development in deaf and hard-of-hearing children.

B. Short Answer Type Questions

1. Who is hard-of-hearing? Define.
2. Define deafness.
3. Hearing levels of speech in dB.
4. Explain classification of deafness.
5. Who is aurally handicapped child.

C. Objective Type Question

1. Which is not the type of deafness?
   (*a*) Hard-of- hearing (*b*) Otitis media
   (*c*) Partial sighted (*d*) Aphasia

SUGGESTED READINGS

1. Best, H. (1943). *Deafness and Deaf in United States*, The Macmillan Company, New York.
2. Cruick Shank, W.M. (1955). *The Psychology of Exceptional Children and Youth*, Staple Press, London.
3. Greenfield, P. and Smith, H. (1976). *The Structure of Communication in Early Language Development*, New York, Academic Press.
4. Hannat, E. and Gardner, M. (1974). *Preschool Language Screening Test, North Ridge*, Calif, Joyce Publication.
5. Hewett, F.N.M. and Forness, S.R. (1977). *Education of Exceptional Learners* in Boston, Allyn and Bacon Inc.
6. Kirk, S.A. (1970). *Educating Exceptional Children*, New Delhi, Oxford and I B H Publishing Co.

4

Orthopaedically and Other Health Impaired Individuals

Orthopaedically children/individuals are highly visible with their movements, speech problems, use of wheel chairs and braces that may evoke a variety of emotional responses in others. One of the most persistent myths regarding exceptional individuals is that a crippled body and crippled mind invariably go together. Individuals with other health impairments, such as asthma, or a heart condition, may be indistinguishable from normal children intellectually, but their lowered vitality, inability to participate in strenuous school activities, and frequent absences may greatly interfere with their education.

Definition

According to Law

Orthopaedically impaired 'means' a severe orthopaedic impairment which adversely affect a child's educational performance. The term includes impairments caused by:

1. Congenital anomaly (*e.g.* club foot, absence of some members of body etc.)
2. Disease (*e.g.* poliomyelitis, bone tuberculosis etc.)
3. Other causes (*e.g.* cerebral palsy, amputation and fractures or burns which cause contractures)

Other Health Impaired

"Other health impaired means limited strength, or alertness due to chronic or acute health problems such as a heart condition, tuberculosis, rheumatic fever, nephritis, asthma, sickle cell anemia, haemophilia, epilepsy, lead poisoning, leukaemia or diabetes which adversely affect child's educational performance."

As mentioned in the above definitions, we have a very diverse group of individuals and within each type of disability condition there is further diversity. Each individual in each type of diversity is unique, as in the case of exceptional learners. We would like to discuss here the individuals with orthopaedic and other health impairments. We include the following disability in individual cases.

Type of Disability

The Impairment that Affect the Individual Motorically

The conditions that affect the individual motorically include:

1. Cerebral palsy
2. Spina bifida
3. Muscular dystrophy
4. Limb deficiency
5. Legg-calve-perthes disease
6. Osteogenesis imperfecta
7. Juvenile rheumatoid arthritis
8. Physical trauma.

Cerebral Palsy (CP)

Bobath and Bobath (1975) defined cerebral palsy, 'as the general category of motor handicaps that involve an impairment of the co-ordination of muscle action with an inability to maintain normal postures and balance and to perform normal movements and skills.' There are four types of cerebral palsy.

1. *Spasticity:* Muscle tightens from increased muscles.
2. *Arthetosis:* Uncontrollable, involuntary, rhythmic movements.
3. *Ataxia:* Muscular incoordination related to balance.
4. *Mixed Condition:* Various combinations of the first three types.

In addition, the particular limit(s) involved and the degree of severity of the paralysis is also categorised:

Mono—One limb.
Para—Both legs.
Hemi—both limbs on the same side of the body.
di—All four extremities with greater involvement in the legs.
quad—all four extremities.

These terms as prefixes for the terms plegia (total paralysis) and paresis (partial paralysis).

1. *Cerebral Palsy:* Cerebral palsy is caused by events before, during or after birth that lead to an injury to the brain. There is a greater risk of cerebral palsy for children born prematurely born during a difficult labour, who experience anoxia during birth (lack of sufficient oxygen) and who sustain head injuries during their early years.
2. *Spina Bifida:* It is a congenital defect resulting in a portion of the special cords not being covered by the vertebrae. The effects of this special cord defect range minor/sensory and motor handicaps to paraplegia and loss of bladder and bowel control. Another effect may hydrocephaly (swelling of the head) due to excessive fluid in the cranial cavity.
3. *Muscular Dystrophy:* One childhood form of muscular dystrophy called pseudo hypertrophies is inherited, progressive and terminal. The disease weakens muscles, resulting in crippling as the affected muscles supporting the skeleton contract and cease functioning.
   The effect of this disease—The walking becomes increasingly difficult, and confinement to a wheelchair eventually necessary.
4. *Limb Deficiency:* A large number of babies whose mother had taken thalidomide during pregnancy were born with malformed or missing limb in 1960 in Europe. To eradicate effect, a tranquilizer prescribed for many pregnant women in Europe. In addition to a condition present at birth, limb deficiency can result from amputation.
5. *Legg-Calve-Perthes Disease:* This disease affects the head of the femur or bone that fits into the hip socket and hampers the ability to walk. The cause of it unknown, but it may be genetic or it may occur as a result of an injury to the upper leg or hip. Treatment involves wearing a brace.
6. *Osteogenesis Imperfecta:* This disease appears to be congenital and is also known as 'brittle bones'. It renders bone growth defective in both length and thickness, and dwarfism and deafness may occur.
7. *Juvenile Rheumatoid Arthritis:* Arthritis results in the deterioration of the living of the joints and can be both painful and deforming. Afflicted individuals may develop fevers, rashes and morning stiffness. Children who suffer may have problems in school because it is painful for them to sit for

long periods of time and difficult for them to write. It is very necessary to mention that administration of polio vaccine on a routine basis to most children in their early years has all but eliminated polio as a cause of orthopaedic problems.

8. *Traumatic Conditions:* Accidents are responsible for the largest number of impairments due to physical trauma.

Other Health Impairments

Besides orthopaedic impairments, there are many more diseases and problems that lead to health impairments. A few of them are being chosen to discuss here.

1. *Seizure Disorders Epilepsy:* Epilepsy has been drawn from the Greek word 'Epilepsia', which means 'a taking hold of a something seizing the subject, as though that something were outside himself.' This definition describes the most pronounced feature of epilepsy, a disturbance in the electrochemical activity of the discharging cells of the brain, which results in a seizure.

   Symptoms: During the actual seizure–

   (i) the child may exhibit a rolling and jerking of the eyes.
   (ii) rapid pulse movements.
   (iii) changing facial colour
   (iv) teeth gnashing.
   (v) laborious breathing
   (vi) Uttering of a shrill cry
   (vii) Beginning of spasmodic movements
   (viii) Convulsions of the body

   This may be followed by drowsiness, headache or nausea. Unconsciousness may be prolonged but seldom for more than half an hour.

2. *Cystic Fibrosis:* It is the result of an unborn error of metabolism that affects the body's ability to produce saliva, perspiration and mucus.

3. *Sickle–Cell Anemia:* It is a heredity disorder, the shape of red blood cells is changed into crescent or 'sickle' that prevents the cell from passing normally through the blood vessels. During a 'crisis' situation, the blood and oxygen supply are abruptly cut off in various parts of the body. Causing severe pain, swelling of the joints, fatigue and fever.

4. *Juvenile Diabetes Mellitus:* The disease is often hereditary

metabolic disorder involving failure of the pancreas to produce enough insulin and maintain a proper balance between sugar and starch and the body's energy needs.

5. *Hemophilia:* This disease involves a genetic blood disorder in which there is a poor clotting ability. Consequently, minor cut and bruises can be very hazardous.
6. *Asthma:* Asthma is usually caused by an allergic disorder and can affect practically every organ and tissue of the body. This creates tissue sensitivity and a predisposition to an allergic reaction.
7. *Cancer*
8. *Cardiac Conditions:* Health impaired children are apt to appear in any regular or special classroom. The teachers need to be aware of the most common health impairments of childhood that can cause lowered vitality, lack of alertness, and frequent absences.

Flexibility Characteristics

Orthopaedic and other health impairments may greatly limit exploration of the environment and the satisfaction of natural interests in jumping, running, holding climbing, throwing and catching, children whose movement or vitality is restricted may be deviced the simple but meaningful experiences. Such restrictions might lead are to believe that ordinary or extraordinary physical activities can never be entered into by individuals with orthopaedic or health impairments. In recent years, it became more and more apparent that such is not the case as the news media have covered some truly remarkable accomplishments.

The flexibility of Orthopaedic and health impaired individuals may be sharply curtailed but when we read of such accomplishments, it may be realized that how the range and nature of experience may combine to challenge many held beliefs regarding limits for the handicapped.

Social Problems of Orthopaedic and Health Impairment

Many social problems of such children results from the impact of others' reactions to the handicap, the individuals interpretation of these reactions and conflicts that arise between the child's aspiration level and his/her actual capacity. The visibility of a handicap has been shown to be related to rejection by others that negatively affect the self-concept of an orthopaedically impaired individual. The adjustment is related more closely to the social impact of the impairment rather than the actual impairment itself.

Intellectual Levels of Orthopaedically or Other Health Impaired Individuals

Cerebral-palsied children did not differ in verbal ability but were inferior on performance items requiring visual motor co-ordination. Frequent absences, lack of stamina and general discouragement accompanying other health impairments can have negative consequences on school achievement. There are the studies which indicate that the greater the severity of the condition, the greater the extent of under achievement, even after age and I.Q. have been taken into account.

Educational Provisions

The individual who suffer from orthopaedic impairment often have a difficult adjustment in approaching adult life. Individuals with cerebral palsy whose handicap is largely confined to the legs, a number of occupations are possible (Schonell, 1969). These include watch repairing, optical or dental mechanics .... etc. The major problems facing individuals with seizures disorders in later life relate to adjustment and exclusion from employment.

The type of programme for the Orthopaedic impairment children largely depends on the extent of the handicap. Home education only be provided if the child has normal or near normal intelligence and is severely physically disabled. Hospitals, schools offer short-term diagnostic and treatment periods during which special education is provided, long-term care is available in institutions for the mentally retarded, where totally dependent children with all degrees of physical handicaps may reside on a twenty-four hours basis. However, the majority of children who have mild handicaps and normal intelligence are generally found in regular public and government school classrooms, where slight modifications in school buildings and classrooms can be made to accommodate their physical impairments.

Orthopaedic impairments often restrict children to special education programmes because of the physical facilities necessary to accommodate them. Once they can maneuver successfully in the school environment, children having such problems may equal or excel their non-handicapped peers in learning.

There has been a lot of progress in India during recent years for the education of the Orthopaedic impaired children. Many schools in urban cities have started to provide many unusual features that include medical and therapeutic equipments to meet with the educational and physical needs of such individuals. Such children should also be given vocational training. Maximum efforts must be made to assist the children in the school by the teachers in view of their family background, such informations must be collected by them.

QUESTIONS

A. Long Answer Type Questions

1. What do you mean by orthopaedically handicapped children? What measures may be taken while educating them?
2. Describe various types of orthopaedic impairment and their causes in short.
3. Describe various types of health impairments. How can they be controlled?

B. Short Answer Type of Questions

1. Who is orthopaedically impaired?
2. Who is health impaired?
3. Discuss cerebral palsy (C.P.).
4. What do you mean by limb deficiency?
5. Seizure disorders and their symptoms.

C. Objective Type of Questions

1. Match List I with List II

List I	*List II*
(a) The shape of red blood cells is changed into a crescent	1. Juvenile diabetes mellitus
(b) Failure of the Pancreas to produce enough insulin	2. Asthma
(c) Genetic blood disorder having poor clotting ability	3. Hemophilia
(d) Allergic disorder	4. Sickle–cell anemia

2. The epilepsy which means a taking hold of a something seizing. True/False
3. It is a kind of disorder (hereditary) in which the shape of red blood cells is changed into crescent
   (a) Juvenile diabetes mellitus *(b)* Sickle-cell anemia
   (c) Hemophilia *(d)* Asthma

SUGGESTED READINGS

Linek, L.J., Shower, J. and Jacob, E.E., *Teaching Orthopedically Handicapped and Cardiopathic,* Forty-ninth Year Book, Part II, pp. 194-215.

Telford, C.W. (1977), The *Exceptional Children,* New Jersey, Prentice Hall Inc.

5

Speech Impaired Children

It is true that speech is the tool which is used to develop and express language. However, it must be known that speech and language are not synonymous, but speech certainly involves language. A child's first speech is one of the most momentous events in human development. Being able to communicate with others in language opens up a storehouse of new information and opportunities. Successful and appropriate language use is linked closely to mastery of social situations, so the inability to understand and communicate with others can hamper a person's ability to cope with even the simplest problems and therefore language defects may be considered speech defects.

Definition of Speech Impairment

'Speech impaired' means a communication disorder, such as stuttering, impaired articulation, language impairment, or a voice impairment, which adversely affects a child's educational performance.

Classification

According to Eisenson (1980), 'speech is significantly defective, when the amount of distraction is sufficient to make it difficult to communicate with normal listener.' Speech defects may be classified as (1) Defects of articulation, (2) Defects of voice and (3) Stuttering and stammering.

1. Disorders of Articulation

Disorders of articulation involve: *(a)* Substitutions, *(b)* omissions, *(c)* distortions and *(d)* additions of sounds. Typical substitution are 'w' for 'r' (as in wight for right). Such errors are commonly found among young children with immature speech.

Omissions tend to make a child's speech almost unintelligible, because consonants are often dropped from the beginning, middle, or ending of words.

Distortions in speech reflect an attempt to approximate a correct sound such as 'whistling'. There are more readily corrected than are substitutions problems. Omissions are difficult to correct.

Additions appear in unintelligible speech and Jargon and in the speech of deaf children who may say sumber for 'summer' or add a vowel between other syllables as 'on a the table'.

2. *Voice Defects*

Voice defects are not found as often as articulation defects. They include problems in (1) Vocal quality, (2) Vocal pitch and (3) Vocal intensity.

Defects in vocal quality appear in the production of sound and include breathiness, hoarseness, or huskiness. Resonance of sound may occur largely in the nasal cavity producing a nasal, twangy quality, outside the nasal cavity it may produce 'spring has cob' instead of 'spring has come'. Since the growing larynx may develop at a faster rate than the rest of the body, pitch may remain at a high level into adolescence. The intensity, loudness, or softness of the voice may reflect attention seeking, lack of control of vocal power, or immaturity or insecurity.

3. *Stuttering and Stammering*

Both these defects have received more study than any other speech problem. It is generally considered disorders of rhythm or fluency. Stuttering is a speech disorder that involves blocking or repetition of, or sometimes a struggling with speech sounds. The term stuttering is synonymous with older term stammering which has gradually been fallen into disuse. However, both stuttering and stammering are two major speech defects. In stuttering, a person speaks with involuntary pauses while in stammering, a person repeats the first letter and stretches it without any control.

The speaking behaviour of the stutterer may vary from mild difficulty with initial syllables of certain words, as in 'D-d-d-don't do that, to violent distortion and momentary inability to utter any sound at all. Most stutterers can speak fluently under ordinary circumstances; the blocking tends to occur at moments of important or stressful communication.

The entire performance of the stutterer represent an 'internal struggle' to speak. After the momentary disturbance, speech becomes smooth and fluent until the next stumbling block. The stutterer's difficulty may vary considerably from one situation to another. Typically, stuttering increases both in severity and frequency in situation where the stutter feels inferior, self-conscious or anxious.

Sheehan (1970) on the basis of his studies pointed out that for the child or adult who has developed the problem called stuttering, the production of spoken word and can be fraught with dread and difficulty. Certainly one can empathize with the young stutterer in the classroom who is eager to answer a question but fears the humiliation and ridicule his stuttering may elicit.

Causal Factors of Stuttering

Stuttering has proved to be a most baffling disorder, attempts to explain it have largely focussed on the following factors:

(i) Genetic and Neurological Factors

Johnson (1961) compared a large group of children who stuttered with a matched group of non-stutterers. He found that a times as many of the stutterers had siblings of parents—mostly fathers—who also stuttered. In a more recent review of research findings, Sheehan and Costly (1975) concluded that genetic factors do play a significant role in the etiology of stuttering. However, these investigators did not rule out the key role of learning in the 'familial transmission' of stuttering. Brain damage causes a different type of speech or language disorder called aphasia, it is defined as a loss or impairment of ability to use language because of brain lesions.

(ii) Learning and Stress

Most of the investigators place strong emphasis on the role of learning and stress as primary causal factors in stuttering. Any stressful situations that lead to severe feelings of inadequacy, self-consciousness, anxiety, fear, and tension tend to impair psychomotor co-ordination and performance and this also includes speech functions. Most of us have experiences blocking of thoughts and speech in stage fright or in situations where we have had to make unexpected introductions. In these situations it is probably to say that we were self-conscious and tense. Defective responses under these conditions are very common.

(iii) Role Behaviour

Sheehan (1970) and Sheehan and Lyon (1974) have pointed to the potential importance of role behaviour and stated that it may take two different forms, but the eventual result is the same.

In the first form the stutter plays a 'false role', in that he attempts to conceal his stuttering, as by assuming a foreign accent or a regional dialect. Even when this enables him to deceive other about his being a stutter at least temporarily, he is likely to experience guilt or doubt. These feelings in turn, lead him to work even harder at denying his role as a stutter and concentrating on his false role as a normal speaker. His false role sooner or later fails in its protective function.

In the second form, the person simply views himself as a stutterer and hence plays that role, 'I am a stutter' becomes a permanent part of his self-concept—a view that is reinforced each time stuttering occurs.

Sheehan makes it clear that accepting the fact that one is a stutterer may have either positive or negative effects. If a person views his stuttering as self-devaluating and a chronic affliction about which he can do nothing, the result is negative. On the other hand, in accepting the fact that he is a stutterer, he has defined his problems, it is important that he does not feel devaluated or obligated to play the role of stutterer. Therapy now-a-days places a strong emphasis on self-acceptance, but not on self-resignation. There may be other causes of stuttering such as:

- *(i)* disharmony of nerves and muscles which may be treated as neurological cause,
- *(ii)* fear of the situation,
- *(iii)* too much strictness in removing the habit of left handedness,
- *(iv)* imitating others,
- *(v)* difficulty in breathing and pronunciation,

(vi) over strictness in removing habit of thumb sucking and other considered as bad habits, and

(vii) Faulty parent–child relationships have been viewed as one cause of stuttering. Some studies show that parents of stutters set unrealistic goals for their children and are over protective and controlling.

Identification and Diagnosis

The identification of the child with a speech handicap may originate in the school as a result of either a brief screening of every child enrolled or a teacher referral. As the pupil is identified having speech problem, he/she may be evaluated by the professionals concerned with various aspects of speech and language. Such an evaluation aims at assessing:

1. variable outside the speech and language are that may relate to the problem, including hearing impairment, intellectual deficits and behaviour disorders, and
2. the ability of the child to produce and to comprehend the language of the culture.

Articulation may be assessed by both spontaneous and imitative tests. In a spontaneous test, the child is shown pictures of familiar objects, events, or people and asked to name or describe them. An imitative test is one in which the examiner asks the child to repeat words, phrases or sentences containing particular sounds with which he/she may have difficulty.

Treatment and Educational Provisions

The treatment for stuttering has taken varied forms such as:

1. aversive conditioning
2. desensitization
3. rhythmic exercises
4. assertion training
5. hypnosis
6. social reinforcement of fluency, and
7. delay of auditory feedback.

These methods fall into two general categories:

1. those involving direct elimination of the stuttering and
2. those involving acceptance and then elimination.

Aversive conditioning and the delay of auditory feedback fall into the first category, here the attempt is made to achieve fluency by means of some special technique, with the hope that this fluency will generalize to the individual life situation. The second approach is based on the view that stuttering is an approach-avoidance conflict generated by certain situations viewed as stressful by the stutterer. In such circumstances desensitization, self-assertion, reinforcement and other thereby approaches may be brought into use.

Appropriate treatment may relieve most stutterers of therapy symptom.

The formal speech therapy is only one type of intervention to place the pre-school child who demonstrates an articulation disorder in a treatment problem. An alternative is to work with the child's parents to help them understand the problem and give their specific suggestions for aiding the child with articulation problems in the home. Another alternative is to have speech therapist work with the teacher to initiate a speech stimulation programme in pre-school or kindergarten.

QUESTIONS

A. Long Answer Type Questions

1. Who is speech impaired child? Classify and explain.
2. Define speech impairment. Discuss disorders of articulation with suitable examples.
3. Discuss 'stuttering', what are its causal factors?
4. How can speech impaired child be identified and diagnosed? Discuss.
5. Discuss various forms of treatment. Explain anyone in brief.

B. Short Answer Type Questions

1. Discuss educational provisions for a speech impaired child.
2. Aversive conditioning as a treatment of stutterer.
3. Identification of speech impaired child.
4. Role behaviour.
5. Learning and stress.

C. Objective Type Questions

1. Stutterer speaks with involuntary pauses. True/False
2. Stammerer repeats the first letter and stretches it without any control. True/False
3. 'D-d-d- don't do' is an example of stutterer. True/False

4. 'Speech impaired' means a communication disorder. True/False
5. Speech is not a tool to develop and express language. True/False

SUGGESTED READINGS

1. F M. Hewett & Steven R. Forness (1984). *Education of Exceptional Learners'*, Allyn and Bacon, Inc. London (3rd ed).
2. Heck, A.O. (1940). *Education of Exceptional Children*, New York, McGraw Hill.
3. Skinner, C.E. (1968). *Educational Psychology* (4th ed), New Delhi, Prentice-Hall of India.

6

Learning-Disabled Children

There are some children in the schools who seem normal but they face difficulty in learning, recalling, copying, writing, listening, understanding and communicating. Their educational performance becomes poor. They require special attention in the classroom from the teacher.

Who is a Learning-Disabled Child?

Children who are quite normal and yet at all times display learning problems. They write 'dab' for 'bad' and 'saw 'for 'was' and unable to concentrate if there is a bit of noise. The National Advisory Committee on Handicapped Children (USA) defined learning disabled children as follows:

'Learning-Disabled Children (LDC) exhibit disorder in one or more basic psychological process involved in understanding and is using spoken or written language. The disorder is manifested in listening, thinking, talking, reading, writing, spelling and arithmetic. They include conditions which are referred to as perceptual problems, brain injury, minimal brain dysfunction, dyslexia and aphasia etc. They do not include learning problems which are primarily due to usual, hearing or motor handicaps, mental retardation, emotional disturbance or environmental disadvantage.'

Above mentioned definition reveals the fact that learning disability is an interdisciplinary area and it is accepted to professionals. However, this definition has been changed and proposed another definition by the National Joint Committee for Learning Disabilities (NJCLD, 1981). In 1985, the Federal Inter

Agency Committee modified the (NJCLD) concept and defined the LDC concept as follows:

Learning-disabilities is a genetic term that refers to a heterogeneous group of disorders manifested by significant difficulties in the acquistic and use of listening, speaking, reading, writing, reasoning or mathematical abilities or of social skills. These disorders are intermixed to the individual and presumed to be due to central nervous system dysfunction. Even though a learning disability may occur concomitantly with other handicapping conditions or socio-environmental influences and especially with attention deficit disorders, all of which may cause learning problems, a learning disability is not the result of those conditions or influences (Learner, 1905).

The above two definitions are similar and indicate that;

Learning-disability was and are unable to concentrate if there is a bit of noise. The National Advisory Committee on Handicapped Children (U.S.A.) defined it as –

Learning-disabled children (LDC) exhibit disorder in one or more basic psychological process involved in understanding and in using spoken or written language. The disorder is manifested in listening, thinking, may or may not be caused by central nervous system.

LDC have significant problems in learning academic skills that are not due to other handicapped conditions.

There are many students with LDC have a lower intelligence than average.

There are many students who have high intelligence and sometimes reach the range of gifted.

The first definition of learning-disability which gained wide acceptance was proposed by Kirk in 1962. He defined it as:

'A learning-disability refers to a retardation disorder, or delayed development in one or more of the processes of speech, language, reading, spelling, writing or arithmetic resulting from a possible cerebral dysfunction and/or emotional or behavioural disturbance and not from mental retardation, sensory deprivation or cultural or instructional factors.'

The two most important things to consider when attempting to identify a child as learning disabled are: (1) Discrepancy, and (2) Exclusion.

Discrepancy

There is significant discrepancy between the child's actual intellectual ability and the level of academic functioning exhibited.

Exclusion

The child does not have any other primary handicapping conditions (underlying the learning problems), such as visual hearing, motor handicaps, mental retardation, emotional disturbance or environmental, cultural or economic disadvantage.

These two criteria serve only a 'bare bones' reference for defining a learning disability but they are to introduce this type of exceptional learner.

Identification of Learning-disabled Children

1. Discrepancy between ability and achievement.
2. Poor academic achievement.
3. Variation in performance in different field.
4. They are impulsive in behaviour while talking and doing activity.
5. Unable to concentrate on one activity.
6. Easily distractible.
7. Faulty perception.
8. Poor memory.
9. Unable to understand oral message.
10. Get easily disturbed.

Perceptual Characteristics of Disabled Children

The learners with learning-disabilities are no more likely to have usual acuity problems as compared to normal children. The problems that are exhibited in visual perception may be result of difficulty in maintaining attraction to visual stimuli and selecting the relevant from the irrelevant (Bryan and Bryan, 1975). It may occur only where applied linguistic stimuli such as letters and words (Vellutino, 1979). Similarly, problems in auditory perception manifested by learning-disabled children, it may relate to difficulty in discriminating auditory content when it is embedded in relevant stimuli. Such problems may be a function of how a child uses and remember the information rather than a function of basic perception or discrimination of sound.

The problem of the child with a learning disability are often most visible and disruptive in the confines to the classroom. If one follows such a child to the playground, to his or her neighbourhood or into the house and then consider how flexible the child is in adapting to the larger environment. It may be observed that the hyperactivity is the most commonly recognized characteristics of children with learning-disability (Traver and Hallahan, 1974). In a review of twenty-one experimental studies of attention deficits in learning-disabled children revealed that hyperactivity might be situationally specific with higher levels of activity being exhibited in structured situations such as classroom.

Cruickshank (1967) in describing such children included hyperactivity along with hyper distractibility, disinherity and impulsivity under general problem heading of distractibility. He felt that the basic difficulty stemmed from the child's inability to refrain from reacting to extraneous external internal stimuli. As a result such a child is often a poor participant in games which require prolonged concentration and attention; he or she is readily drawn away by distracting noise and activity or by irrelevant thought about past or future events. Empirical studies on attention deficits reveal that children with learning-disabilities are deficient in their ability to maintain attention over prolonged periods of time (Krupski, 1981).

Traver and Hallahan (1974) conducted an experimental study on ability to attend to visual signal. Results indicated that the learning-disabled children tended to commit more impulsive errors and to respondless quickly correct than did their non-disabled peers.

Clements and Peters (1962) found in his study that parents of children with learning-disabilities often express concern with the child's tendency to 'not concentrate for more than a few minutes at a time', 'to jump from one thing to another' and 'not to mind everybody's business but his own'.

Stewart (1970) interviewed with mothers of hyperactive children and mothers of normal children and found that hyperactive youngsters exhibit a number of problems at home.

The Psycho-educational Perspective

The psycho-educational perspective focuses on to what the child can or cannot do in learning.

(*a*) *Perceptual Disorders:* The child who reads aloud the word 'saw' as 'was' is demonstrating a perceptual problem when we pass a visual screening test with flying colours but still have problems during the process of seeing a certain stimulus and reacting to or perceiving it. Such problems are found among children considered learning-disabled.

(*b*) *Attention:* Studies with children considered learning-disabled have revealed that many have attention disorders (Douglas, 1972; Sykes, *et al.*, 1971-72). These disorders may involve problems in coming to attention, or focusing, sustaining attention or vigilance, and decision-making based on rapid or impulsive attending behaviour (Keoghs and Margolis, 1976).

(*c*) *Memory and Information Processing:* The problems to learning-disability may occur not only because the child fails to receive adequate information in one or the other sensory modalities but also because he or she fails to relate such information to an existing information array or previously learned material.

(*d*) *Psycho-linguistic or Oral Language Disorders:* Such a learning-disabled child has problems 'using language' and an 'imperfect ability to listen'. Individuals may have difficulty in expressing themselves and using sentences that are fragmented or more like expressions of younger children (expressive language disorder). Some children may have inner language disorders and have difficulty in thinking in an organized and in accurate manner. Vellutino (1970) has suggested that subtle disorders in speech or language are actually one major cause of learning-disabilities particularly in reading.

(*e*) *Written Language Disorders:* Such disorders refer to, 'an imperfect ability to read, write, spell' or do ' mathematical calculations' as characteristics associated with the learning-disability. From the medical point of view, these disabilities are referred to as:

1. Dyslexia (reading-disability).
2. Dyscalculia (mathematical disability).
3. Dysgraphia (spelling and written language-disability).
4. Strepphosymbolia (reversing letters in writing or reading *i.e.*, on for no, was for saw).

The Medical-Neurological Perspective

From Brain Injury to Minimal Brain Dysfunction

From a medical perspective, children who have a very severe reading problems, are diagnosed as suffering from 'word blindness', and the notion that such problems may have a neurological basis. This notion got support from Hinshelwood in 1917, when he differentiated between adults who had lost his ability to read (acquired word blindness or alexia) and children who were unable or who had great difficulty to read (congenital word blindness or dyslexia). Strauss and Werner identified two contrasting groups of mentally retarded children. One group was made up of children for whom there was no explanation for their retardation except that they 'born that way '. The other group consisted of children whose retardation was thought to be the result of a brain injury at some time during their lives although both groups' children were clearly retarded, the brain injured group could be identified by their *(a)* hyperactivity, *(b)* perseveration (tendency to pursue a single task past the point when most individuals would stop), *(c)* Perceptual disorders, *(d)* distractibility, and *(e)* emotionality. Children who exhibited such behaviour were found from among brain injured damaged group.

The most frequent characteristics of children label MBD (Minimal Brain Dysfunction). The hyperactive child does random, purposeless and extraneous movements that are situational inappropriate (Schworn, 1982).

Intellectual Characteristics of Learning-Disabled Children

Intelligence of these children typically has a range from low average to average on individual intelligence tests (Benton, 1972; Vellutino, 1979). The discrepancy between their normal intelligence and their academic achievement as measured by achievement tests becomes the benchmark of learning disabilities. Subtle impairment in linguistic functioning may be a possible factor associated with learning-disabilities and it becomes clear that undetected problems in both language and information processing may be characteristics of a large number of learning disabled children (Hesler and Kitchen, 1980).

In respect of memory, many such children are passive learners, they do not use strategies (rehearsal or mnemonics cues) (Hallanhan *et al.*, 1985). Learning-disabled children display certain characteristics as regards remembering:

1. They feel difficulty in assimilating, storage and retrieval of information.
2. They have difficulties in reproducing rhythm patterns, sequences of digits, words or phrases.
3. They have difficulty to see the relationship between his present and past experience.
4. STM and LTM of the learning-disabled children are poor.
5. Regarding to reading nearly 25 to 90 per cent of learning-disabled children have poor academic achievements that include mispronunciation, skipping, adding or substituting words (Lloyd, 1985).

Social Characteristics of Learning-Disabled Individuals

Researches suggest that parents, teachers and peers alike often view them negatively (Bryan & Bryan, 1978). The following results have been obtained:

1. Parents have described their children as clinging but unable to receive affection.
2. Disabled children show little control in both emotional and motor expression.
3. They show trouble in listening and expressing themselves. Teachers have been found to view these children as behaviourally less desirable in the classroom than the normal children.
4. They show less consideration for others.
5. Teachers judge these children as less competent in following direction, comprehension in class discussion, vocabulary, time concepts and general coordination.
6. They are rated lower on:

   (a) cooperation,
   (b) paying attention,
   (c) organizing themselves,
   (d) coping with new situation,
   (e) being socially accepting,
   (f) acceptance on responsibility,
   (g) completing assignments, and
   (h) being tactful.

It was found in a study conducted by Keogh, *et al.*, (1974) on teachers perceptions on learning-disabled and educable mentally retarded children that teachers tended to view retarded children primarily as educationally problematic while teachers viewed LDC as have earning, behavioural and personality problems. When compared to normal children of the class LDC appear to be significantly less popular and more rejected by their peers if the LDC is female (Bryan, 1974b).

Learning-disabled children's academic retardation may continue to a lower self-concept. In a study conducted by Black (1974) found that the LDC with reading retardation viewed themselves more negatively than similar with normal reading achievement, the greater the underachievement, the poorer the self concept. Observational analyses of classroom situations indicate that these children's social life in classroom differs from that of others (Bryan and Wheeler, 1972).

Causes of Learning- Disabled Children

The actual cause of a learning disability is unknown. However genetic, organic, biochemical, developmental and environmental causes have been postulated.

1. The persistence of severe reading problems within succeeding generations of the same family has provided evidence of a possible genetic source (Lewitter, 1975).
2. Complications during the birth process such as anoxia (oxygen deficit) can cause neurological impairment, injuries to the head and certain diseases such as measles and encephalitis that produce an extremely high body temperature.
3. Environmental causes of learning-disabilities have been explored. Severe malnutrition at an early age can actually alter a child's learning capacity as can an impoverished range of experience or lack of environmental stimulation.
4. Emotional or behavioural problems may produce such learning disability characteristics as inattention and hyperactivity and motivational deficits common among children who have experienced continual failure may do the same.
5. Inadequate instruction in the early grades may create problems for the child that will be viewed later as indicators of a learning disability (Adleman, 1971).

Educational Provisions

Education for learning-disabled children consists primarily of three types.

1. *Special Section in a Regular School:* There should be a special class for such students as they require special instruction by special teacher but regular classroom teacher should also assist in teaching subject contents. At the same these children must receive instruction on academic subject in special class but socially they should be provided opportunity to interact with general students.
2. *Day School*: In such school, the LDCs are segregated from the general students. They receive here specialized schooling using special teachers essentially the same curriculum but greater care.
3. *Main Streaming:* LDCs who do not pose organic problems or the problems of low intelligence are integrated in the regular classroom having resource room facilities.

Following general instructional techniques have been used and recommended to educate learning–disabled children.

1. Short, brief direction and large print help these children. Teacher should keep this fact in mind.
2. Consistent language and colour cues will help them to understand the content.
3. Diagram or pictorial illustrations proved very helpful to increase their knowledge.
4. All the steps or directions should be written on the chalkboard and important portions, words should be underlined.

Some Main Problems of LDC

1. Poor Handwriting

Poor handwriting among the learning-disabled children has been attributed to numerous causes *e.g.* *(a)* poor motor control, *(b)* poor eye and hand coordination, *(c)* poor visual discrimination.

A creative teacher improves handwriting using certain techniques keeping in view the student's capabilities and their skills.

2. Spelling

Spelling errors are quite common among learning-disabled children.

In view of it a systematic work-study technique is used in the following sequence:

—"Look at the word—say the word—look at the word—read the word—write the word—check your spelling—Repeat."

Students may be asked to spell the word properly and clap softly for each vowel sound. It may be used to correct spelling. This technique is called remedial technique.

3. Arithmetic

Ashlock (1972) made certain remedial.

Instruction steps for removing arithmetical errors for learning-disabled children. Some of the steps are as follows:

1. Use manipulative such as buttons and chips to teach numbers.
2. Use visual materials and give reinforcement.
3. Use graph papers for alignment difficulties.
4. Time line, coloured chalks, markings are helpful for attention to cues.
5. Sample problems should be given for each assignment.
6. Avoid distraction as far as possible.
7. Use of displayed charts, playing cards, calculator, language marking are quite useful.

Approaches to Teach Learning-Disabled Children

1. *The Cognitive Processing Approach:* This is "how a child learns and offers a frame work for teaching."
2. *The Developmental Approach:* This stresses on sequential way for remediation. Hierarchy to be developed in its using criterion referenced teaching. Published matter may also be used for remediation of LDC.
3. *The Test Related Approach*: It identifies specific field area of deficiency which can be modified.
4. *The Specialized Technique Approach:* This approach indicates that the teacher would follow the prescribed order and fashion for a specified period of time.
5. *The Behavioural Approach:* It refers to behaviour modification approach for manipulation of environmental conditions of learning. Success of this approach depends upon the suitable application of reinforcement.

A teacher can use one or more of the different approaches to deal with the situation. Koppitz (1973) advocated:

"..................learning disabilities can not be corrected or cured by a specific teaching method or training technique. It is imperative that teachers have a wide range of instructional materials and techniques at their disposal and that they are imaginative and flexible enough to adapt these to specific needs of their pupils."

QUESTIONS

A. Long Answer Type Questions

1. Who is learning-disabled child? Discuss various methods of identifying such children.
2. Discuss various characteristics and problems of the LDC. Suggest a plan for their education.
3. Define "LDC". Evaluate critically its different causes. Suggest some preventive measures.

B. Short Answer Type Questions

1. Discuss programs to educate LDC.
2. Discuss the advantages and disadvantages of special classes.
3. Discuss various causes of LDC.
4. Distinguish between LDC and normal child.

C. Objective Type Questions

1. Exceptional children's needs are very different from those of the majority of children in society. True / False
2. LDC are.
   1. Academically superior 2. Hyperactive

   (*a*) 1 is correct (*b*) 2 is correct
   (*c*) 1 and 2 are correct (*d*) 1 and 2 are incorrect
3. LDC have a positive self concept. True / False

SUGGESTED READINGS

1. Backer, H.J. (1944). *Introduction to Exceptional Children*, New York, Macmillan.
2. Heck, A.O., (1940). *Education of Exceptional Children*, New York, McGraw Hill.
3. Hewett, F.M. with Forness, S.R. (1984). *Education of Exceptional Learners*, (3rd ed.), Allyn and Bacon, Inc.

7

Emotionally Disturbed Children

There are a few children who are emotionally disturbed due to the lack of recognition, favour shown to others, and the lack of affection from their parents and teachers. They can be well recognised with the help of sociometric tests, personality tests, rating scales and anecdotal records etc. Experienced teachers can easily identify such children. There are various reasons of their disturbances like uncongenial environment of the school, strange behaviour of the parents and teachers, poor socio-economic status and low mental ability. However only 'seriously emotionally disturbed' children/individuals are eligible for special education services.

Definition

Seriously emotionally disturbed is defined as follows:

1. The terms mean a condition exhibiting one or more of the following characteristics over a long period of time and to a marked degree, which adversely affects educational performance.
   - *(a)* An inability to learn which cannot be by intellectual sensory, or health factors.
   - *(b)* An inability to build or maintain satisfactory interpersonal relationships with peers and teachers.
   - *(c)* Inappropriate types of behaviour or feelings under normal circumstances.
   - *(d)* A general pervasive mood of unhappiness or depression.
   - *(e)* A tendency to develop physical symptoms or fears associated with personal or school problems.

2. The term includes children who are schizophrenic or autistic. The term does not include children who are socially maladjusted unless it is determined that they are seriously emotionally disturbed.

One thing is to remember that mildly and moderately disturbed children are excluded from being in this category because:

(a) The behaviour of the mildly and moderately disturbed children exists largely in the eyes of the beholder.

(b) The behaviour of mildly and moderately disturbed children may be transient in nature, being observed in some children in the early grades but not later on.

One of the authors has attempted to define emotional disturbance 'as consisting of problem behaviours that are negative variants of six levels of learning competence, attention response, order, exploratory, social and mastery (Hewett and Taylor, 1980). These levels of competence are necessary for any effective learning to take place. Their acquisition makes the normal learner normal; their non-acquisition makes the disturbed learner disturbed. The levels can be defined as follows:

1. *Attention:* The level of competence associated with receiving and perceiving sensory stimulation coming to and sustaining attention and retention.
2. *Response:* The level of competence associated with motor responding, verbal language skills and active participation.
3. *Order:* The level of competence associated with following directions and routines.
4. *Exploratory:* The level of competence associated with gaining an accurate and thorough knowledge of the environment through sensory motor experiences.
5. *Social:* The level of competence associated with gaining the approval and avoiding the disapproval of others.
6. *Mastery:* The level of competence associated with self -help skills, academic skills and vocational and career development.

The above six levels of learning competences considered as optimal. Each level of behaviours that constitutes negative variant, consisting of, 'too little' of the competence or 'too much' of the competence.

Now we are able to define emotionally disturbed behaviours as 'consisting of biploar deviations from optimal behaviours required', for learning (too little or too much of a good thing.

Too little ←——— Optimal ———→ too much

Deviant Normal Deviant

Table–7.1

Common characteristics of disturbed children behaviour problem Quary and Peterson (1975) viewed as negative variants of six levels of learning competence:

Too little	Optimal	Too much
Disturbance in sensory Perception	Attention	Fixation on particular stimuli
Immobilization	Response (Motor)	Self-stimulation
Failure to develop speech	Response (Verbal)	Extremely talkative uses profanity verbally abusive
Self-injurious lawlessness	Order	Very confirming resistance to change, compulsive
Bizarre or stereotyped behaviour	Exploratory	Tries to do everything at once
Pre-occupation with inanimate objects, extreme self-isolation, inability to relate to people	Social	Inability to function alone
Blunted, uneven or fragmented Intellectual development	Mastery	Over intellectualization

Table–7.2

The Behaviour problem (Quary, Peterson 1975), Behavioural characteristics of disturbed children as negative variants of six levels of learning competence.

Symptoms of behaviour Too little	Optimal (1) Attention	Symptoms of behaviour too much
1. Excessive day dreaming		Selective attention
2. Poor memory		
3. Short attention span		
	(2a) (Response Motor)	
1. Sluggishness		*(i)* Hyperactive
2. Passivity		*(ii)* Restlessness

3. Drowsiness
4. Clumsy
5. Depression

(2b) Response (verbal)

Failure to use language for Communication	1. Extremely talkative

(3) Order

1. Descriptiveness	1. Overly conforming
2. Attention seeking	
3. Irresponsibility	
4. Disobedience	

(4) Exploratory

1. Anxious	1. Plunges into activities
2. Pre-occupation	
3. Does not know how to have fun	
4. Behaves like adult	
5. Shyness	

(5) Social

1. Social withdrawal	1. Hyper sensitivity
2. Alienates others	2. Jealousy
3. Aloofness	3. Overly dependent
4. Prefer younger playmates	
5. Acts bossy	
6. Secretiveness	
7. Sighting	
8. Temper tantrum	

(6) Mastery

1. Lacks self-care skills, Basic school skills	1. pre-occupation with academics
2. Laziness in school	
3. Dislike for school	
4. Lacks vocational skill	

Werry (1979) is of the opinion that there are two type of severe emotional disturbance or psychoses that exist.

1. *Schizophrenic Disorders:* Regression or arrest in development after a period of relatively healthy development. Schizophrenic children (onset 5-12 years of age) have some useful language and are able to relate at some level to others.
2. *Early Infantile Autism:* Two primary symptoms: *(i)* extreme self-isolation and an obsessive insistence on sameness, *(ii)*

if consists of speech and language disorders which range from mutism to echolalia (repeating what others say rather than initiating spontaneous speech), (Onset 0-2 ½ years of age.

Identification and Diagnosis

The common criteria on which is commonly used to identify emotionally disturbed children is the judgement of the class room teacher. A teacher who is familiar with the typical range of learning and behavioural differences found among children in a certain age group is in a better position to single out children with special problems. Harth and Glavin (1971) conducted a study in which significant correlation between teacher ratings of 'disturbed' behaviour and the result of the individually administered California Test of personality, designed to measure adjustment problems among children, have been found. Earlier studies have also revealed that teachers were surprisingly accurate in their designations of emotionally disturbed children when their selections were compared to those made by psychologists and psychiatrists (Bower, 1960; Bower, 1961). A Psychologist may also administer projective personality test such as Rorschach, TAT aimed at getting children to reveal inner conflicts.

The identification of psychotic children may be made early in life as their parents become aware of the serious discrepancy between their functioning levels and those of other children of their age. Frequently, the first professional contact with a pediatrician or psychiatrist is the result of parental concern when the child fails to develop speech or exhibit unusual speech patterns.

Schizophrenic children usually have serious language problems and communicate poorly. They may exhibit their narrow interest and seek a sameness in the conditions of their environment, some times they are pre-occupied with one object such as a particular toy.

Infantile autism is a more extreme condition than schizophrenia although behaviour expression in both cases may be the similar. There are two features that distinguish autism from schizophrenia are the age of onset (autism is usually present at birth whereas schizophremia develops in early childhood) and the autistic individuals' failure to develop typical schizophrenic symptoms such as hallucinations and delusions in later life (Eisenberg and Kanner, 1956).

Disorders of Childhood

Attention-Deficit Hyperactivity Disorder (ADHD)

It is often referred to as hyperactivity, it is characterized by difficulties that interfere with effective task-oriented behaviour in children particularly impulsivity, excessive motor activity and difficulties in sustaining attention. The disorder occurs most frequently among preadolescent boys and it is six to nine times more prevalent among boys than girls DSM (IV) ADHD occurs with the greatest frequency before age eight and tends to become less frequent and with briefer episodes thereafter. Some residual effects such as attention difficulties may persist into adolescence or adulthood. Hyperactive children usually have great difficulties in getting alongwith their parents because they do not obey rules.

Causal Factors in ADHD

The potential genetic basis has not been firmly established, although there is some support for the idea that it is a familial disorder (Faraone *et al.*, 1994a). Environmental factor (home) is influential in the development of the disorder.

Anxiety Disorders of Childhood and Adolescence

Anxiety disorders are apparently quite common in the general population. Two anxiety disorders of children and adolescence (1) separation anxiety disorder and (2) selective mutism.

1. *Separation Anxiety Disorder:* It is the most common of the childhood anxiety disorder. This is exhibited by the children *i.e.* school refusal problems (a fear of learning home and parents to attend school) and continue to have adjustment difficulty overtime and make difficult work and life adjustment later.
2. *Selective Mutism:* Another anxiety disorder some times found in childhood is selective mutism a condition that involves the persistent failure to speak in specific social situations *e.g.* in school or in social groups and is considered to interfere with educational or social adjustment.

   Both genetic and learning factors have been cited as possible causal factors underlying the disorder. Family-based psychological treatment is the most common therapeutic approach used.
3. *Childhood Depression:* It includes behaviours such as

withdrawal, crying, avoidance of eye contact, physical complaints, poor appetite, and even aggressive behaviour. There appears to be an association between parental depression and behavioural and mood problem in children. Learning maladaptive behaviours appears to be important in childhood depressive disorders (Kaslow *et al.*, 1994).

4. *Autism (Pervasive Developmental Disorder):* Autism is a developmental disorder that involves a wide range of problematic behaviours including deficit in language, perceptional and motor development, defective reality testing, and an inability to function in social situations. Autism in infancy and childhood was first described by Kanner (1943).

Autist Children have following Characteristics

1. *A Social Deficit:* Such children do not show any need for affection or contact with anyone, usually not even seeming to know or care who their parents are.
2. *An Absence of Speech:* The absence of or severely restricted use of speech is characteristic of autistic children, who have been considered to have an imitative deficit and do not effectively learn by imitation (Smith and Bryson, 1994).
3. *Self Stimulation:* Usually taking the form of such repetitive movements as head banging, spinning, and rocking, which may continue by the hour.
4. *Intellectual Ability:* Autistic children are skilled at fitting objects together. Thus their performance on puzzles or form boards may be average or above. Even in the manipulation of objects, however, difficulty with meaning is apparent.

Causes

The causes of a child to become emotionally disturbed, is often depend one one's own point of view, however there may be six point of view.

1. *Developmental:* A normal child may on occasion exhibit serious problem behaviours. But their frequency of occurrence, degree of severity, duration, and clustering fall within limits that are acceptable to the child's environment and those within it. During the course of growing up, we are all exposed to stresses and strains, frustrations unpleasantness and pain. But these times are over shadowed

by the times we are relaxed loving, happy, confident and content. If frustrations and disappoints fall out of limits that may not be acceptable to the child, it may lead the child to be emotionally disturbed.

2. *Temperamental:* The negative nature of experience that may cause can result in the child's developing emotional and behavioural problems. The children who are 'wall climbers' can create havoc in a family of sedate 'seat sitters'. The problem can occur between a child predisposed to a low activity level and family members who are always on the go and who are constantly impatient with their child's lethargic behaviour.
3. *Biological:* Biological factors to the development of emotional disturbance is strongest in relation in schizophrenia and autism. There is no conclusive evidence linking such factors to the vast majority of mildly disturbed children (Kaufman, 1977).
4. *Psychodynamic:* From a psychodynamic perspective, emotional disturbance results from the child's failure to withstand the psychological strain produced by critical adjustment periods during early childhood. These adjustment periods center around feeding, wearing, toilet training or the development of sexual awareness.
5. *Behavioural:* The causes mentioned above of emotional disturbance generally focused on 'in-child' issues. In contrast, the behavioural approach concentrates on outside child issues, such as the relationship of agents and events in the child's environment to observable maladaptive behaviours. In this view, such behaviours are the result of reinforcement and punishment.
6. *Ecological:* There is no side taking with respect to the importance given 'in-child' *versus* 'outside-child' issues. The focus is on the child's interactions that have occurred or are occurring between the child and all aspects of his/her environment. The home and family are components of the ecosystem, as are the school and teachers.

Flexibility Characteristics of Severely Emotionally Disturbed Children

Children with respect to deficit in reception and perception of sensory stimuli. Ornitz and Ritvo (1968) postulate that such children may suffer from inability to maintain perceptional constancy *i.e.* they do not perceive identical experiences in the same way each time they occur. The behaviours of such children suggest that they get too much or too little input from the environment. Some emotionally disturbed children approach the activities and experiences of childhood at home, in the neighbourhood, and in school with impulsive, uncontrolled behaviour, others draw away, preferring to remain uninvolved, isolated, and withdrawn.

Intellectual Characteristics of Severely Emotionally Disturbed Children

Research related to the academic progress of disturbed children reveals consistent evidence that they do not perform in line with their intelligence (Forness *et al.*, 1983).

'Well-behaved' boys were found to score significantly higher than those with 'behavioural problems' on the verbal intelligence test (Woody, 1968).

Treatment and Educational Provisions

The following appraisal and intervention have been involved in efforts to help disturbed children.

1. Medication
2. Psycho-therapy
3. Behaviour modification
4. Ecological.

1. Medication

Medication has been found effective for some emotionally disturbed individuals. Schain *et al.* (1975) found that psycho stimulant drugs are useful to increase teachability and manageability from 50 to 80 per cent of hyperactive children.

2. Psycho-therapy

Psycho-therapy or some form of counselling may be recommended for disturbed children.

3. Behaviour Modification

Behaviour modification approaches to the treatment of the severely disturbed is currently being used by many practitioners. Unlike psycho-therapy behaviour thereby very specifically defines its treatment, techniques and goals. In this technique therapist concentrates on observable behaviour and assumes an active role, reinforcing adaptive behaviours that the child displays and ignoring or punishing maladaptive behaviours immediately after their occurrence. This technique has been successful in increasing attention and reducing problem behaviours.

Educational programmes for severely emotionally disturbed children usually focus on individual or small group activities. Speech and language training are often the primary concerns, alongwith self care and social skills.

4. *Ecological*

The ecological approach conceptualized disturbed children as needing to be 're-educated' rather than 'treated' and set up 24 hours groups homes where children attend school, work, play and live with special educators. A typical Re-Ed (Re-educable) unit consists of eight children and three key adults – two teacher counsellors and one liaison counsellor. The teacher counsellors operate the daily programme, the liaison counsellor examines and explores each of the eight children's ecosystems. The home schools are visited and conferences held with the home teachers. The children's families are counselled.

QUESTIONS

A. Long Answer Type Questions

1. Who is emotionally disturbed child? Discuss the characteristics of seriously emotionally disturbed child.
2. Define emotional disturbance. Discuss various levels of learning competence.
3. Discuss common characteristics of disturbed children viewed as negative variants of six levels of learning competence.
4. Discuss behavioural characteristics of severely disturbed children viewed as negative variants of six levels of learning competence.

B. Short Answer Type Questions

1. Two major types of severe emotional disturbance or psychosis.
2. Identification of emotional disturbed child.
3. Discuss disorders of childhood.
4. Discuss childhood depression.
5. Autism.

C. Objective Type Questions

1. A social deficit is one of the characteristic of pervasive developmental disorder. True/False

2. Autism is a developmental disorder that include deficit in language. True/False
3. The causes of a child's emotionally disturbance depend on one's own point of view. True/False
4. Treatment of emotionally disturbed child involves effort to help
   (1) Medication (2) Ecological
   (a) 1 is correct 2 is wrong *(b)* 2 is correct 1 is wrong
   (c) both are correct *(d)* both are wrong
5. Behaviour modification has no place on the treatment of emotionally disturbed children. True/False

SUGGESTED READINGS

1. Barnes, T. and Forness, S.R. (1982). Learning Characteristics of Children and Adolescents with Various Psychiatric Diagnosis'. In R. Rutherford & A Prieto (Eds). *Severe Behaviour Disorders of Children and Youth* (Vol. 5), Reston, Vs. Council for Children with Behaviour Disorders.
2. Coleman, J.C. (1972). *Abnormal Psychology and Modern Life* (4th ed.) Glenview, III, Scott, Foresman and Co.
3. Greenfield, P. and Smith, H. (1976). *The Structure of Communication in Early Long Development,* New York, Academic Press.
4. Hewett, F.N.M. and Forness, S.R. (1977). *Education of Exceptional Learners,* Boston Allyn and Bacon Inc.
5. Roy S. Dutta (1980). *Psychological Disorders of Young Children,* New Delhi, Sterling Publishers Pvt. Ltd.
6. Forness, S.R. (1981). *Concept of School Learning and Behaviour Disorders,* Implications for Research and Practice, Exceptional Children 48, 56-64 (b).
7. Forness, S.R., Benett, L. & Tose, J. (1983). Academic deficits in emotionally disturbed children revisited. *Journal of Child Psychiatry,* pp. 22, 140-44.

8
Disadvantaged Children

There is no primary dimension of such disadvantaged children but have possible related dimensions such as vision hearing, movement, perceptual, motor-communication and social-emotional dimensions. Recent years it has been witnessed increasingly public concern with the plight of the socially disadvantaged. Psychologists and sociologists have long been interested in possible differences between children of varied social and economic background. They have played important and significant role in translating this into practical knowledge. Psychologists who are interested in the various aspects of human development tried to understand the relationship between developments and factors unique to the disadvantaged. They are also involved in various remedial efforts.

Poverty is one of the oldest and most important and widespread of all handicapped conditions. It has also constituted more of a problem for certain racial and ethnic groups than for others. Although not all poor people are from ethnic minorities and not all socially or culturally different individuals are poor. Children may be exceptional learners because of poverty or socially or culturally unique backgrounds or a combination of the two. Economically disadvantaged and/or a socially or culturally different children have had a variety of euphemisms applied to them such as it is said that they live in *jhuggi's* and *jhompris*, inner city or in disadvantaged community. They are often labeled deprived and disadvantaged and their cultural patterns are viewed as inferior or deficient.

Meaning and Concept of Disadvantaged/Deprived Children

The word 'deprivation' has been derived from the verb 'deprive' which means to 'dispossess' or strip person or an object and it implies a felt loss. In other words it may be stated that absence of any opportunity or freedom provided by society or nature to individuals. Tribe persons living in backward areas or interior places may be included in this category as they are away from getting certain normal opportunities provided to others. The term disadvantage and deprivation are used interchangeable but there is little difference between the two. Disadvantage is a broader term which means unfavourable conditions and circumstances, detriment, loss injury or prejudice so it includes all types of physical handicaps while deprivation is narrow and restricted concept. It is referred only to circumstances which become obstacle for the natural development of inner potentialities of the child. It is also fact that deprivation may be for short duration for others and may also be for long duration.

Environmental psychologists proved this fact with the help of their studies that development of the individual is the result of interaction between individual's inherited endowments and the environment. A number of studies have been conducted on the development of deprived/disadvantaged children's personality. The deprivation is universal. It is not restricted to any race, community, caste, religion or place. It has a wider perspective and meaning for the scheduled tribes and scheduled castes for India. Deprived children are the end products of the social, economical, and cultural disparities in their relative societies. There are various groups in every society who are living in a very unhygienic condition and are deprived of the pre-requisites for their development. Deprivation is referred to the non-availability of desired experiences not the membership of any group. According to Garden (1965),'deprivation is a deficiency of stimulating state of childhood.'

Bolman (1973) defined, 'deprivation indicates low life status or separation which stops the persons from taking part in their cultural achievements of society.'

Ruth, Dass and Dass (1979) stated three symptoms of deprived children:

1. gradual delay in and intellectual development,
2. gradual delay in educational achievement, and
3. closing of immature educational period.

Characteristics of Disadvantaged/Deprived Children

1. They are economically poor. Actually they are the product of poverty or more accurately they are caught up in the self-perpetuating cycle of poverty and failure. The factors that prevent them from moving into the mainstream of socially are:
    - *(a)* crowded and inadequate housing,
    - *(b)* high rate of illness and malnutrition,
    - *(c)* family instability,
    - *(d)* delinquency, and
    - *(e)* crime.
2. Many of the disadvantaged are exposed to prejudices commonly inflicted upon minority groups. More important is their background in terms of language; customs and attitudes may subtly prepare them for a life different from that of the middle class.
3. Many such children do not complete their academic or vocational training and in turn are unemployed or under employed Poverty leads a person on the following situations such as:
    - *(a)* Poor maternal health, growth, nutrition and poor supervision.
    - *(b)* Elevates infant mortality, morbidity and family size.
    - *(c)* Malnutrition illness and absence of medical care.
    - *(d)* Social deprivation and environmental inadequacy.
    - *(e)* Increases rise of school failure.

All the above factors affect on being unemployed and under employed and these are experienced by disadvantaged/deprived individuals.

Role of Expectancy and Self-Concept

Teachers' interaction with children for whom high and low success expected plays a significant role in the performance. Brophy and Good (1970) conducted a study and found that teachers who have high expectations from those pupil are more likely to praise on their correct answers, less likely criticize on their wrong answers and more likely to provide some kind of feed back after each answer Such a teacher's behaviour improved future performance of those thought to be higher achievers and conversely depressed the relative standing of those from whom little was expected because achievement expectancy is usually for the disadvantaged as teachers' behaviour work against them.

Aside from being influenced by expectations of others, performance is also shaped by self-expectancy. If a group whom the disadvantaged children belong, is disliked or looked down upon by the members of society who relatively have unfavourable image about them or stereotyped ideas which have negative effect on their performance, however for this the individuals must be aware of being a member of disliked group. The evidences whatever available indicate that this awareness occurs early usually before the age of four and that the tendency is more pronounced among minority group members.

Low self-esteem leads to poorer performance that in turn perpetuates low self-esteem. Rosenberg (1965) found that students who did not achieve high grades in school typically had relatively low self-images and low occupational expectations. In addition to it they frequently described themselves as withdrawn, overly sensitive and suspicious such traits of personality are not likely lead experiences of success that might improve their self-concept.

Family Structure and Disadvantaged Children

Poverty is an important factor *i.e.,* individuals with inadequate income are harassed constantly by the financial worries and tensions strain marital bonds. Besides it the disadvantaged are frequently powerless to change the factors that affect on their livelihood or save money for emergencies or for improvements. It is also reasonable to assume that children who are growing up in absence of father are deprived of a relevant model for identification.

Child's neglect is associated with low socio-economic status, one-parent family structure and a large number of children. It has been studied that poverty is not an invariant commitment of neglect rather implications is that poverty exposes parents to the increased likelihood of additional stress that may have deleterious effects upon their capacities to care adequately for their children [Giovannoni and Billingsley, (1971)].

Language of the Disadvantaged Group

If we compare the language of middle and lower class youngsters frequently have resulted in conclusion that the lower class child is considerably deficient in many aspects of language development such as sentence length, vocabulary, grammar and syntax. It has been known fact that language does not only serve communicative function but also involved in thinking.

One investigator Basis Bernstein (1962) distinguished between restricted and elaborated language codes and explained that reliance upon the former by lower class children limit their learning of conceptual skills. In restricted language there is a dependence upon a relatively small number of words and phrases. There is also a little attempt to communicate fine ideas or feelings. Middle class children are capable of using a restricted code but also possess an elaborated structure of language with which they can express themselves more precisely. It has been found out that lacking an elaborated code lower class children have difficulty in developing and applying abstract ideas. He also predicted that their power of analysis would also be handicapped by their language. However Robinson disagrees with this theory argues that lower-class individuals are able to speak either in elaborated or restricted codes. He concluded that the differences reside in their type of speech used in everyday life rather than in any inability to use elaborated language.

Types of Deprived/Disadvantaged Children

There are three major types of such children:

1. Emotionally Disadvantaged or Deprived.
2. Culturally Deprived or Disadvantaged.
3. Economically Deprived or Disadvantaged.

1. Emotionally Deprived or Disadvantaged Children

Psychologists have supported this fact that the first few years of a child in the family are known as the formative years for his future life. Parents communicate their affection to their child and deal him/her according to their own ways regardless of their status, culture, religion or custom. Every child wants to be loved and to be understood. He may feel secure; get recognition and importance, which he receives, from their parents, grand parents and other members of his/her family. This relationship with the child has profound effect on the physical as well as mental health of the child; it is with in this framework that the child gets his/her first experience emotion of love and hate, happiness and anger, fear and surprise and joy and sorrow. This is an important aspect for the foundation stone of development of personality *i.e.*, emotional adjustment is laid in the family. If a child does not experience all this behaviour in the family he may think himself-herself emotionally disadvantaged or deprived.

2. Culturally Disadvantaged or Deprived

The term 'culture' describes the whole way of life that is learnt, held in common and passed on from one generation to another by members of a particular society. In modern days the people of a particular society belonging to the main stream presume that their culture is the best and others are deprived of the culture. People belonging to scheduled caste and tribes are culturally deprived as they have been living for centuries under conditions of intense social disadvantage and were prevented from sharing in the social- cultural life of the mainstream. They lack of schooling and other progressive programmes added to their plight. They were deprived of both materialistic gains as well as intellectual pursuits. These people's social living is not congenial for their growth and rightfully development of their creative ideas, higher values and goals. They are superstitious; they have primitive social livings, customs and crude manners.

3. Economic Deprivation

Economic deprivation and poverty are synonymous. Poverty is a cluster of factors leading to general lack resources to fulfill of their needs.

Effects of Deprivation

Each type of deprivation affects on the growth and development of the person such as:

Motivational and Emotional Development

A deprived child has low level of motivation and his/her aspiration is also very poor, he or she does not get appreciation from the members of the society for the achievements that the child deserves. As indicated earlier if a child does not get affection, love, and belongingness from his/her parents especially from mother, he or she is unable to develop lovable and dependable relationship with adults. Deprivation of parental love may affect a child' intellectual, social and physical development.

Language, Cognitive Development and School Achievement

(a) *Limited Verbal Communication:* Parents of the deprived children are mostly uneducated have little time or ability to develop the necessary language skills among their children through conversation, creative discussion and to solve their curiosity.

(b) *Slower Cognitive Development:* Cognitive development refers to the development of those mental processes which enable the child to acquire knowledge of himself/herself and the world around. Knowledge grows out of experiences but parents of such children are unable to provide a variety of objects which may enrich their experiences and help to develop their cognitive ability.

(c) *Lower Scholastic Attainment:* Various studies have indicated that there is high positive correlation between parental socio-economic status and scholastic attainment. Children who belong to rich families are found to have generally higher attainment scores than their counter parts from poor families.

(d) *Self-concept and Personality:* Self-concept is meant as to how one perceives oneself in comparison to others in particular situation. The development of child's attitude *i.e.* construction or destruction, acceptance or rejection, toward himself/herself and others depends on the parents and others attitude toward him or her.

Negative concept have been found to manifest negative self-concept among children from deprived homes as their life result in forming a cluster attitudes that express low self-esteem, neglect, a sense of inefficiency and insignificance.

Personality traits that are generally associated with deprived children are fear from challenges which they are unable to face. They develop negative attitude towards adults, teachers' and school. They blame their poor performance on the world as a whole rather to blame themselves. They sometimes blame for their unsuccessful performance on their fate.

Social Class, Child Rearing and Cognitive Development

Most of the children spend most of their early childhood in the company of their parents. The child rearing practices are to exercise great influence on their future development. However, the families of different S.E.S. vary in their modes of interaction, their children are to be expected to develop in some what different directions and at different rates as well. Kohn (1963) noted that one of the chief differences between the occupations of the lower and middle classes is the way they foster either self-direction or compliance. The lower class occupations place more emphasis on manipulation of concrete things than on abstract ideas and interpersonal relations. They are more likely to be supervised and routinized and to depend upon group efforts rather than individual initiative. Parents of lower class may carry these experiences over to the way in which they control their youngsters.

According to Hess and Shipman, lower class families status oriented *i.e.* they accept the *status quo* and passive compliance to rules as unquestionable and appropriate. Status orientation underlies the restrictive mode of dealing with the world that is taught through mother- child interaction. Middle class families, in contrast, are hypothesized to be person oriented because this approach emphasizes attention to individual feelings and roles; it leads to consideration of alternatives and variations rather than simple rule obedience. The difference in language use between the middle-class mother and those of the other groups when they interacted with their youngsters. Middle class mothers had greater verbal output, spoke with more abstract words and used more complete sentence structure as compared with lower class mothers who have consistent view of restrictiveness of cognitive modes.

Causes of Disadvantaged/Deprived Children

Although poverty may be the major determiner of disadvantage, its specific effect on the child that leads to educational problems. Followings are some other causes of disadvantaged group of children.

1. The Bio-medical Position

Insufficient medical care and nutrition before and after birth and impoverished living conditions may greatly limit the ability of disadvantaged children to function successfully in school (Birch and Gussow, 1970).

(a) *Malnutrition:* Severe malnutrition in infancy and chronic under nutrition from birth into the school years may result in information-process deficits and accounts for the lack of attention, apathy, irritability and lower energy levels often displayed by disadvantaged children.

(b) *The Impoverished Conditions*: The unsafe conditions slum environment make the child more susceptible to injuries and the absence of recreation areas increase the probability of accidents.

2. The Cultural Deficit Position

The limited range of experience of disadvantaged child is viewed as the explanation for frequent school failure. This is the cultural deficit position, and it focuses on the disorganized and impoverished physical family environment of the child. Such an environment is to be understood as failing to provide the quality of sensory, social and language stimulation necessary for normal cognitive development.

3. The Cultural Difference Position

The cultural deficit position has been challenged by the proponents of the culture difference approach in explaining the learning problems of the disadvantaged in school. Cole and Bruner (1972) are of the opinion that the disadvantaged child possesses the same basic competence as a middle counterpart but the two express their competence in different ways. It all depends upon the situation or environment which a disadvantaged child faces in interaction, however if the same child is given the environment according to their culture, he becomes excited and starts conversation and demonstrate superior reasoning and debating skills.

Identification of Disadvantaged Children

Disadvantaged have variety criterion for identification such as

1. low family income.
2. ethnic minority group status.
3. deteriorated housing.
4. urban or isolated rural living environments.
5. poor over all performance.
6. poor reading skill.
7. limited language skill.
8. low scores on standardized intelligence and achievement tests.

Disadvantaged children also exhibit certain psychological characteristics related to their school problems.

1. They give up easily and to fail to display drives for achievement.
2. They express feelings of powerlessness and possess a poor self-concept.
3. They have problems in delaying gratification and are more motivated to work for external rewards such as money than for internal rewards such as the satisfaction of acquiring knowledge and skill.

Educational Provisions

The School and the Disadvantaged Students

A disadvantaged student is likely to be poorly prepared to enter and to progress in the traditional school settings. He is likely to be handicapped in approaching academic tasks requiring a variety of basic cognitive abilities (Coleman, 1966). It is because his language development is limited as it is restricted in form, serving to communicate and generally confining thinking to a relatively low level of repetitiveness (Bern Stem, 1962).

Social class differences in language associated with social class tend to increase with the age of the child, as he grows older, he falls further and further behind middle class children. The acquisition of language is a prerequisite to concept formation and problem solving thus language deficiency would certainly indicate a tremendous lower-class deficit in conceptual function.

Disadvantaged children tend to depend more on real life encounters than on symbolic experiences in developing ideas and skills. Their functioning tends to be slower, their time orientation is shorter and their ability to attend to and concentrate on sustained academic tasks poorer.

They are likely to be less highly motivated and to have lower aspiration for academic achievement than middle-class children and receive little academic encouragement from either parents or peers.

The Teacher and the Disadvantaged Student

As we know that disadvantaged students encounter greater difficulties in learning, they need special skills and understanding on the part of the teacher as they may be exposed to the most highly trained and experienced teacher within school system. A study conducted by Symonds showed that the need for achievement, inherent in the teacher frequently gave rise personality problems and clashes in class room. This need to achieve on part of middle-class oriented teacher is often frustrated when teachers attempt to put achievement into operational effect in the deprived school or class rooms. The middle class is also likely to be confused with the behaviour of children whose whole cultural background differs so widely from his/her own.

If the teachers from the ranks of the under privileged are recruited, there is no guarantee such teachers would be truly oriented to the needs and problems of the disadvantaged children. In a significant number such cases, the lower-class individual who violates class expectancies by becoming a teacher does so because of his/her dedication to stereotyped middle-class values and a need for upward social mobility. Consequently despite his background, he may adopt middle-class expectations of his pupils that are not unlike those of middle-class teachers.

What is needed? If our rapidly changing society is to remain viable, we can no longer afford a *laissez faire* approach to the education of culturally and economically disadvantaged children. Consequently it is essential to provide maximal educational opportunities consistent with the youngsters' abilities and potential for all such children. Thus education must be geared to the actual needs—intellectual, social and vocational—of the child especially the disadvantaged child.

We can provide better schools for deprived children as the school is the single social institution most involving all children represents the best opportunity for breaking the relentless cycle of the 'culture of poverty' and the institutionalization of separate but unequal ways of life for the deprived children.

We do not only need but most essential part is to provide all the physical facilities and equipments as well as. We also need a 'total push' approach to upgrade the educational effort directed at the children of poverty in order to bring them up to a level at which they can profit by more traditional learning experiences.

It is to be noted here that it is difficult to tell which kind of programmes would be most productive. The most significant and important thing at this juncture is to experiment on a broad scale and to construct and build into such efforts which may be adequate means of evaluation. If any kind of programmes to have any hope of being successful, and if such programme is to become capable of being applied on a wider scale, there would be a great need for upgrading the training of teachers. The teachers require broader training in better understanding of psychological, cultural, intellectual needs and the problems of the disadvantaged, general ways to deal more effectively with them. They would also need specific training in carrying out special curricular programmes. It might also be added that even optimal conditions of training and experience, the teacher need maximum support from administrative and supervisory personnel. It is also true that if the school programmes meant for disadvantaged are to work successfully, teachers must gain the confidence of parents and community.

In this regard an attempt was made to expose the disadvantaged child in which he was given enriched environmental experiences in a view that it would overcome their previous deficits but this programme could not be successful as who were enrolled failed to sustain their acquired intellectual gains in later school years (Spicker, 1971).

Compensatory Education for the Disadvantaged Children

Although education is not a panacea for poverty but it does a lot to ameliorate the situation. Achievement in school is not possible if the opportunities for success are not available. The schools continue as a powerful instrument for social improvement and attempts are to be made to restructure the old and to add innovative programmes. This can be done by changing curriculum, conditions and methods of teaching such as an increase in flexibility, individualized programming, self-instructional materials and emphasis on activities to overcome deficit in language and reading. New programmes may be instituted ranging from extra tutoring after school to enrichment experiences such as visiting museums or attending camps. Teachers should involve parents in the planning and in implementing of the programmes. At present many different compensatory pre-school programmes exist. The innovators of such schools agree that early education is worthwhile and that disadvantaged children can learn under the 'right' conditions keeping in view that motivation is important for learning and that the young child must enjoy school experience. Although state has taken certain legislative administrative measures to ensure their equality and to eradicate discriminations against them by providing certain privileges.

Fein and Clarke Stewart (1973) have identified six dimensions that are not necessarily independent but are very significant to warrant separate consideration.

1. Conception of the Child

The most important and significant of all the dimensions is, how the child is viewed as a human being. At one point it is assumed that children are motivated by their intrinsic forces to grow and learn.

Thus the educational settings should have an enriched environment that allows the children for their self-expression and creativity. This view was influenced by Gesell and Freud. At the other point of the continuum is the environment holds that the intellect is plastic and under the control of the environment, that cognitive and moral knowledge and rules must be learned and that the education occurs from the outside. Between the two extreme forms is the interaction's position which assumes that structural changes occur in the child depending upon world experience.

2. *Goals for the Child*

This dimension, according to Fein and Clarke-Stewart state most easily described by the question, "should the child become an informed being or learned being." The goal of those who want the informed being model is to prepare the child for school by stressing specific knowledge in language, reading and arithmetic. On the other end of the continuum is a focus on the process of learning; the child must learn how to learn rather than acquire specific facts and skills.

3. *Aspects of Development Emphasized the Soft Side of this Dimension*

The programme innovators are most interested in socio-emotional growth. This approach was meant for the nursery school of the past, where it was successful in fostering independence, curiosity, self-reliance and sociability. It was not considered popular model for the pre- schools for the disadvantaged, which focus more on perceptual, cognitive development. Language development is the central point in this domain. Between the extremes of this dimension is the 'whole child' orientation that characterizes present day nursery schools.

4. *Amount of Adult-Child Contact*

Most of the educational programmes are initiated by the teachers and the direct contact between teachers and children vary in a great deal. There are programmes which emphasize more strongly the child's manipulation of material while other programmes emphasize personal interaction with the teacher modelling of certain behaviours being expressed in the classroom and verbal instructions given to the children. In general focus on people rather than material seems to be more successful.

5. *Programme Technique/Degree of Structure*

The technique of education in pre-schools can vary widely from low to high structure. The high structure clearly and rigidly prescribes lessons and the manner in which they are taught. In such programmes the children are kept busy with such prescriptions with a minimum of free time. In contrast low structure pre-schools set no curriculum; they 'let it happen' by providing qualitative personal relationships, a varied environment, opportunity for play experiences and health care. The middle approach espouses a generally unstructured format in which structured lessons are interspersed.

6. *Level of Education Attempted*

Depth of educational system distinguishes pre-schools. There may be a direct approach to change academic and social behaviour exhibited by the child or at other extreme, an effort should be made to build cognitive, affective and social structure. However, their goal can be best achieved by working with the family.

Home *versus* School

From a sociological point of view that focuses on the economic, social and psychological problems which are found in many poor families, in such situation we may apply a social service model in the hope that counselling and guidance would ameliorate the situation thereby it would foster their achievements. If this approach does not become effective we may use another model involving parent as educator, emphasizes mother-child interaction more directly in terms of cognitive growth and social adaptability. Leventein (1970, 75) provided the Verbal–Interaction Programme (VIP) which was based on the foundations from such a base as indicated above. This programme is based on the following fundamental assumptions:

1. Parents are profoundly important as primary agents of change.
2. The mother-child affective-on-going relationship is critical to learning and should be disturbed as little as possible.
3. The ages between two to four years are important as attachment between mother and child peaks because termination of the sensory-motor stage is a peak time for learning.
4. The motivational influence of love or attachment between mother and child will be optimized in a stable situation that encourages language, sensory-motor skills and the child's intrinsic motivation to master the environment in play. It must be kept in mind that mother must be fully aware and completely confident of what was being done to the child.

Mother should be given training sufficiently in this regard by the educational/child psychologists.

Modification of the Effects of Deprivation

Deprivation is a curse for the development of the individual as well as nation; however some remedial measures are given below:

1. Early intervention is more effective than after intervention. Home environment and nursery school atmosphere should be congenial for their cognitive, affective and psychomotor development.
2. Motivational factors bring a lot of changes in their abilities.
3. It is an error to consider that deprived children are globally deficient. Righman (1963) found that they showed cooperative attitudes, formalities and happiness towards their classmates.

According to Ruth (1982) we can modify their achievements by providing them education with the help of the following methods;

1. By making efforts to remove the learning deficits due to the lack of the pre-school environment.
2. By making efforts to remove deficits in the special subjects.
3. By making efforts to fulfill the primary needs of deprived children.

Educational Provisions by the Government

Some enrichment programmes have been designed to develop and enlarge children's conceptual repertoire and communication skills. Some programmes are being practiced in the country; it had very good and effective outcomes although not to the extent as required.

1. Steps have been taken to establish residential schools for such children who cater the needs of the disadvantaged children.
2. Government has taken the initiative to solve the economic problems that exist in these schools. Such residential schools are not sufficient keeping in view of their population. Government is keen to appoint expert teachers to teach disadvantaged children.
3. This problem is being solved rapidly.
4. Poverty is the main cause which is found to be barrier in the

progress of these children. Government is giving financial aid to these students since long.

5. Some useful crafts like carpentry, weaving and tailoring have been introduced to suit the needs of such children which are a must for their development.
6. The percentage of disadvantaged children is high as they come from low SES. As there parents are needy and impoverished. The Government has taken steps to stop this evil of drop-outs by providing incentives so that they would be able to send their wards in schools regularly.
7. The percentage of drop-outs and stagnation can be reduced to the minimum if school hours and vacations can be properly adjusted so that these children may get ample opportunity to help their parents.
8. It is true that educated parents can get their children educated with little efforts. In view of it, measures are being taken to educate illiterate parents through Adult Education Programmes.

QUESTIONS

A. Long Answer Type Questions

1. Who is a deprived child? Discuss the concept of deprivation in the Indian context.
2. What are the objective measures for assessing the deprivation level of children? Explain briefly.
3. What are the cognitive characteristics of disadvantaged/deprived children in the light of researches?
4. What measures should be taken to eliminate deprivational effects on the learning of the children?
5. What educational provisions can be made to educate the socially disadvantaged group?

B. Short Answer Type Question

1. Disadvantaged children and their education.
2. Motivational characteristics of disadvantaged children.
3. Cognitive and perceptual characteristics of deprived children.
4. Meaning of Disadvantaged/deprivation.
5. Problems of socially disadvantaged deprived children.

C. Objective Type Question

1. Socially disadvantaged children must be trained to achieve objectives—1. knowledge, 2. skill, and 3. attitude.
   (*a*) 1 and 2 are correct (*b*) 2 and 3 are correct

(*c*) 1 and 3 are correct (*d*) 1, 2 and 3 are correct.

2. Aspiration level of disadvantaged children should be increased. True/False
3. Self-concept of disadvantaged children is good. True/False
4. Scheduled caste and scheduled tribes are considered as socially disadvantaged children in the school. True/False

SUGGESTED READINGS

1. Ginsberg, H. (1972). *The Myth of the Deprived Child*. New Jersey, Prentice Hall.
2. Misra, G. & Tripathi, L.B. (1980). *Psychological Consequences of Prolonged Deprivation*, Agra, National Psychological Corporation.
3. Mohanty, A.K. and Misra, G. (2000). *Psychology of Poverty and Disadvantages*, New Delhi, Concept Publishing Company.
4. Rath, R., Das, A.S. and Das, U.N. (1979). *Cognitive Abilities and School of Socially Disadvantaged Children in Primary Schools*. New Delhi, Allied Publishers.
5. Sahu, S. (1980). Mediational Deficiency among Disadvantaged Children. *Journal of Social and Economic Studies*, 2 (1) pp. 59-68.

9

Backward Children

There are children in the school who are unable to progress in class according to their age group. They have no interest in learning programmes and avoid taking part in curricular and co-curricular activities. Such children are called educationally backward. However, it is a relative concept which can be used to express any low level achievement in one or more subjects. A child may be backward in academic performance as a whole. It is that specific psychological factor that affects the total development of personality of a child. The key factor of academic backwardness is exclusively seems psychological. Such type of children sometimes becomes problematic due to their frustration and emotional imbalance.

Who are Backward Children?

Backward children are slow learners. They show inability to progress normally in school work. They are unable to do the work of the class in which they are placed or even of the class below that.

According to Schonell, 'if they are compared with other pupils or of the same chronological age, they show marked educational deficiency'.

In other words, it may be stated that a backward child is one who does not progress educationally as per his abilities and lags behind the children of the same age in educational achievement. He is usually a slow learner and proves himself educationally a failure. Therefore, he remains in the same class for years and finds himself unable to do the work of the class next or next below that which is normal for his age. It is to be kept in mind while understanding a backward child that low I.Q. does only neither make a child backward nor a backward child is to be considered a mentally retarded or dull.

In the words of Barton Hall, 'A child may be both dull and backward but he is not necessarily backward because he is dull.'

Cyril Burt defined, 'A backward child is one who is mid-school career is unable to do the work of the class next below that which is normal for his age.' He goes ahead by giving a more precise definition in terms of educational ratio Educational Quotient (E.Q.) *i.e.*

E.Q. = Attainment Age/Chronological Age or A.A./C.A.

Thus a backward is one whose educational ratio is below 85 whereas a medium child has educational ratio or E.Q. between 85 to 155.

One of the most important characteristics of the backwardness is 'educational impoverishment.' Backwardness may be in one or more subjects or in all subjects. Accordingly, we may say that backwardness is two types:

1. General backwardness.
2. Specific backwardness.

General backwardness is due to intellectual deficiency or dullness.

Specific backwardness is due to extrinsic conditions such as-absence from school, ineffective teaching methods or unfavourable temperamental and emotional attitudes towards the teacher/teachers or poor physical conditions.

Scholastic failure, according to Udai Shanker,' is essentially the psychological failure since the simple intellectual experience can not be separated from the total mental life of the child.' Investigations and studies on the problem show that it is not merely an educational problem but it is equally a personal and social problem. They suffer from deep frustrations in life and number of them relapse into delinquency and other anti-social ways of living. Burt is of the view that most of the paupers, criminals and the never-do-wells are recruited from the educationally sub-normal. Many of them become problem children and their behaviour is like a mentally sick or the maladjusted children.

Causes of Backwardness

Research and studies reveal the fact that there are multiple factors that determine as far as the causes of backwardness is concerned. These factors are:

1. *Sub-normal Physical Development:* It has been found that some children are born with an inherited lack of vitality which causes them slow. Burt found 79 per cent of the educationally backward children suffering from some kind of development or physiological retardation.
2. *Physical Defects and Disease:* It all contributes to the causation of scholastic backwardness. Physical defects in a child mean that some of sense organs are not functioning adequately as the first cognitive act in the life of a child is performed through sense perception.
   Schonnel states that 65 to 80 per cent of the backwards are dull or deficient and the remaining 20 per cent have their educational difficulties due to emotional and social maladjustments. This innate dullness limits to understand the content of knowledge or learning or attainment.
3. *Poverty:* Poverty is one of the causes of backwardness. No one can deny this fact damaging effect created by poverty on scholastic achievements. However, there may be exception.
4. *The Emotional and Moral Condition in the Home:* If the homely atmosphere is characterized anxiety, frustration, quarrels and insecurity or parental attitude is too harsh or too indulgent, the children will not be able to develop qualities which are essential for making progress as students.
5. *The Influence of Neighbourhoods.*
6. *Children with Emotionally Disturbed:* Such children are always backward in studies as their mind is agitated and torn by conflict. It may be said that such symptoms come up due to poor parenting. They themselves suffer as stated; "Children are not problem children, but parents are the problem parents."
7. *School Environment:* The environment of school influences on a child's academic achievement. Wrong educational methods, defective and ineffective learning-teaching process, inability to complete homework, the child fails to adapt to classroom teaching-learning process. He lags behind in class. He is not well motivated and inspired to complete his home assignment. Consequently he develops tense relations with the teacher. The highly intelligent students also often

become backward. The schools that have poor educational status because of lack of the proper and required facilities and instruments, defective educational system, indiscipline and mismanagement are also responsible for backwardness among the children.

8. *Family Environment:* The students who belong to low socio-economic status are often very weak in health and they neither get all educational facilities nor car. they have all the experiences and resources available to children belonging to a middle and high socio-economic status. They feel humiliated due to lack of books, exercise books and other required materials. Due to these and other mentioned reasons make them unsuccessful in coping with their classes. The educational status of the parents also affects the children's progress in class. They are unable to get proper guidance from their parents. Parents' unhealthy attitude towards education makes them backward. Parents' education, the family relationship, behaviour of the family members, size of the family, relations with parents, all these factors influence on the child's academic achievement. Frustrations and tensions that are faced by the parents create hindrances in the fulfillment of the child's social and psychological needs. Feeling of security and self esteem do not develop in such an environment. There is always absence of proper motivation and affection at home. He draws his attention away from the education and he becomes a backward.
9. *Faulty Emotional Development:* It is an individual case of backwardness in which the child suffers from such inferiority complex which create hindrances in his academic progress according to his capacities and abilities.
10. *Social and Interpersonal Relations:* There are other innumerable factors in social environment which affect both directly or indirectly on students' achievement such as neighbourhood environment, age of the peer groups, the SES, educational as well as cultural status of the parents.

Characteristics of Backward Children

1. Slow learning children or backward children or educationally sub-normal (ESN) children show a characteristic of weakness in their thinking ability, inability to find out relationship,

similarity, familiarity and have poor development in concept, language and also number concept.

2. They reflect poor verbal ability, their vocabulary is brief, and sentences are very brief and simple.
3. One of the most frequent characteristics of backward children is the weakness of their memory. Burt (1946) remarked – "of all the special mental disabilities that hamper educational progress – the most frequent is a weakness in what may be termed as long term memory."
4. Backward children are very restless and distractible. Poor perception because of poor attention.
5. The learning speed of these children is very slow.
6. They have attitude of pessimism about life. Sometimes they develop the tendency to indulge in anti-social activities.
7. They cannot take benefit from the general school curriculum.
8. They may have a low I.Q.
9. They have no ability to make speedy progress.
10. They are unable to develop higher mental thought processes.

Identification of Backward Children

The correct method of observation and diagnosis is necessary for a teacher in order to identify the backward child. We can use any standardized test of intelligence to assess the intellectual level of the backward child. We can also use some other battery of psychological tests to assess his sensory activity, span of attention, speed and accuracy of hand movements etc. Child's educational characteristics and temperamental traits should also be assessed as certain personality traits have a direct bearing on the specific backwardness. It includes persistence, assertiveness, sensitiveness, approval and disapproval. Diagnosis will not complete unless information about the results of physical and medical examination is also made available.

The Treatment of Backwardness

The main task of a teacher is to assist a particular child to make a proper adjustment to the demand of his situations keeping in view the limits imposed by his circumstances and his natural abilities. Actually treatment depends on the kind of backwardness and the causes which produce it. The school doctor, parents, teachers, social workers and community psychologists should work together in order to identify the correct causes of backwardness and as such proper remedies may be made available. Backward child requires teachers of exceptional efficiency who can adopt suitable teaching methods to teach him. The following treatment may be useful:

1. Regular medical check-up. Physical weaknesses, inefficiency should be brought into the light to the parents and the teachers so that proper treatment may be initiated.
2. Proper guidance by the expert for adjustment. Sometimes the problem of adjustment lead to the mental agony of the children at home and school, that causes avoidance of love, too much neglect or too much affection Expert should provide proper guidance so that they may not develop inferiority complex.
3. *Special Educational Provisions*: It is very difficult to teach such children in normal class, as they are unable to understand that content which is meant for the normal children. Such children should be provided special treatment by introducing the following processes:
   (*a*) Special classes.
   (*b*) Special schools.
   (*c*) Special curriculum.
   (*d*) Special teaching methods.
   (*e*) Special teachers.
   (*f*) Provision of rich experiences and diversified courses.
4. Follow-up programmes and to have progress records.
5. Control of truancy
6. Provisions of Guidance Services.
7. Avoidance of negative environmental factors.
8. *Motivations:* When an improvement in achievement in any field is observed, they should be rewarded psychologically. They require different techniques of motivation. A teacher should instill confidence in such children and continue to make efforts to remove fear of failure.
9. Individual Attention.

Role of the Teacher

A resourceful teacher should follow the effective teaching technique and principle such as:

1. Individual treatment technique should be adopted to teach backward child or slow learners. This principle is known as skilful teaching which is based on knowledge of children's

development and to provide them suitable learning experiences. It is called learning in groups but based on individual needs on the basis of which grouping has been done.

2. Teachers who teach backward children are expected to follow appropriate and effective methods of learning teaching process.
3. Backward children are to be motivated through a sense of satisfaction and achievement.
4. Law of readiness should be applied sincerely. It is the teacher who is to recognize whether the child is ready for the learning prescribed for the stage by systematic observation of his performance.
5. Learning and teaching should be based on meaning, practability and usefulness.

Guidance to the Parents

There are many difficulties that arise due to wrong attitudes developed in the mind of the parents. Parents need advice on how to promote development of their children. They should be given guidance at the right time for the welfare of the children.

QUESTIONS

A. Long Answer Type Questions

1. Who is backward child? Discuss various educational programmes for him.
2. Discuss the difference between a backward child and a normal child. Suggest some remedial measures for him in the classroom situations.
3. Briefly discuss various causes of backwardness.
4. Discuss the attempts that can be made to bring the backward children back to a normal level of achievement.
5. How can a backward child be identified? Discuss various characteristics of backwardness.

B. Short Answer Type Questions

1. What are remedial instructions?
2. Identification of backwardness.
3. What are the characteristics of backward children?
4. What are the causes of backwardness?
5. Discuss educational programmes for backward children?

C. **Objective Type Questions**

1. Backward children's needs are different from those of the majority of children in society. True/False
2. Enrichment triad programme is more popular approach developed by Terman for backward children. True/False
3. Backward children have positive self-concept. True/False

SUGGESTED READINGS

1. Burt, C. (1937). *The Backward Child.* University of London Press, London.
2. Schonell, F.J. (1949). *Backwardness in Basic Subjects,* Oliver and Boyd, London.

10

Delinquent Children

Juvenile delinquency has always been one of the most serious problems of our society. It is basically a legal concept and has been defined in different ways. In our culture, it is generally applied to children under 18 who exhibit behaviour which is punishable by law. It is also observed that most of the delinquents are adolescents when they draw that attention of the authorities; they generally begin their illegal activities during middle childhood (Glueck, 1950).

The word 'delinquency' is generally understood to mean as 'falling away' from normal behaviour. In other words, it may be stated that a delinquent is a person whose behaviour falls always from the existing social norms of the society. According to legal point of view delinquency means certain anti-social behaviour offences committed by adolescents when if committed by adults would be considered as a crime and such acts would be dealt in the court of law and shall be punished accordingly.

Definitions

Good defines, 'Juvenile delinquent is any child whose conduct deviates sufficiently from normal social usage that it may be labelled anti-social.

According to Valentine, 'the term delinquency refers to the breaking of some law.'

Goodwin *et al.*, state, 'Delinquent is a child or youth who repeatedly commits acts which are punishable as crimes.'

C. Burt defines, 'A child to be regarded as technically delinquent when his anti-social tendencies appear too grave that he becomes or ought to become the subject of official action.'

If we analyze, the above mentioned definitions of delinquency, we find that juvenile delinquents deviate from the social or cultural behaviour of the society to such an extents and commit such acts which if committed by an adult would be punishable as crimes.

Forms of Delinquent Behaviour

There are so many types of delinquencies in the schools, it is not possible to examine to all of them. Followings are some of the important delinquent activities which are found in the schools.

1. *Sex Delinquencies:* Such delinquencies do exist in our schools and generally found at the later childhood and adolescence stage. This type of offences may be categorized as offences with opposite sex with willingness as well as unwillingness.
2. *Bullying:* There are some students who are physically stronger than others. They tease and bully the weaker children and force them to participate in some activities which are anti-social.
3. *Stealing:* Some of the children acquire thing of others by stealing as they cannot afford or it may be beyond their means to acquire.
4. *Smoking:* It is a form of delinquency which needs the attention of teachers and parents to handle it psychologically. It is considered as one of the symbol of getting recognition from others which they cannot receive from their normal behaviour.
5. *Truancy:* It is another way of expressing frustration. A student begins to cut classes and absents himself from the school as they are unable to adjust with their fellows, teachers and with the school environment.
6. *Lying:* Children start lying when parents are unable to satisfy their psychological needs. They lie because of fear and escape from punishment. Unhealthy and unsuitable surroundings become responsible for the act of lying.
7. *Wandering:* Sometimes, children wander aimlessly. Teachers and parents are unable to satisfy their curiosity which is repressed consequently their behaviour comes up or expressed through this act.

Causes of Delinquent Behaviour

Various studies have been conducted to find out the factors that are responsible for the onset of delinquent behaviour. The investigations and critical studies reveal the fact that 'delinquents are not born but made.' Although Lambroso believes that hereditary factor is also responsible for delinquent behaviour. Followings are the causes which are considered for delinquent behaviour.

Heredity

It was accepted earlier that delinquency is caused by heredity. Delinquent children inherit this tendency from their parents. The study conducted by Galton, Goddard and the study of Dugdale of the family of Jukes proved that heredity plays part in bringing out delinquency. The factors that are responsible are:

(i) *Defective Families:* Defective members of the family lead to juvenile delinquency. Parents of children suffering from backwardness, lunacy, epilepsy etc., are prone to develop into delinquent children.

(ii) *Phyical Traits:* Lambroso and his colleagues are of the view that the factor responsible for delinquency is heredity. Certain physical defects are transmitted through hereditary and these traits become responsible for delinquent activities.

(iii) *Intelligence:* There is a some large proportion of mentally deficient children among juvenile delinquents than among the population at large. There is wide range of intelligence in the delinquent group (Mussen *et al.*, 1963). Merrill in his study found that average I.Q. of the delinquents was 92.5 as compared with 101.8 for the no delinquents. The average difference between the two groups is not a large one, there is a great deal of overlap between the delinquent and no delinquent groups. Low intelligence, and of itself cannot be considered a major factor in determining most cases of delinquency (Capelin and Siebert, 1964, Conger and Miller, 1966).

(iv) *Emotional Defects:* Most of the delinquents are unable to control their negative emotions. Burt found that main factor responsible for child's delinquency is his innate emotional instability. Due to this drawback children are unable to control their emotions which are not only harmful for

themselves but also create problems to their peers and teachers in the school.

Environmental Causes

Environmentalists are of the opinion that delinquents do not inherit delinquent character from the genes of their parents or ancestors but anti-social behaviour or act is learned from the uncongenial environment, parent-child relation and other social conditions. In this regard, Prof. Udai Shanker (1952) drew a conclusion 'Delinquency is, therefore not inherited; it is the product of social and economical conditions and essentially a coefficient of the friction between the individual and the community. The most important cause of anti-social behaviour are environment and sociological in character.'

Home Environment

Followings are the important aspects of home environment which are responsible for the delinquent behaviour.

(i) *Poverty:* It is stated that 'poverty is the main cause of delinquency'. A family that is suffering from poverty is unable to provide basic amenities to the members. Consequently they satisfy these basic needs through their delinquent acts. A hungry child may cultivate the habit of stealing. Such children generally spend their time outside the home in order in satisfy their basic needs.

(ii) *Broken Home:* Johnson in his study concluded that the delinquent children are from homes where parents died or separated or divorced each other. In such circumstances they do not get sufficient attention recognition and affection at home. The hostile attitude of step father or mother may also lead to frustration, mental conflict and emotional tension. It generally leads to delinquency.

(iii) *Improper Discipline:* Too rigid or too lax discipline in the family leads a child generally to delinquency. If the discipline is too rigid, the child revolts against it. It has been found that girls react passively being submissive while boys react actively and indulge in delinquent activities. If the discipline is too lax, the child gets full freedom to act according to his wishes and may fall in the delinquent activities.

(iv) *Vicious Home Atmosphere:* Sexual immorality, drunkenness, family fighting and quarrelling make homely life vicious.

Parents themselves are responsible to create such an environment, they themselves involve in anti-social activities. In such environment, their offsprings get training to be a delinquent. The children in such families are excited and full of emotional tensions and likely to develop fear and anxiety, consequently discharge their frustrations through wrong doings.

(v) *Parents-child Relationships:* A study conducted by Sheldon and Gluecks (1950) on delinquents and no delinquents revealed that no delinquents were better handled by their parents than the parents of delinquents. Physical punishment was the favourite disciplinary method used by delinquent boy's parents while the no delinquents' parents reasoned with their children more frequently about their misconduct. In general, the delinquents' parents were less affectionate, more indifferent and hostile toward them and showed less warmth, sympathy and affection. In brief, 'the delinquent boys for more than the no delinquents grew up in a family atmosphere which is not conducive to the development of emotionally well-integrated, happy youngsters, conditioned to obedience to legitimate authority (Glueck, 1950).

The apparent role of disturbed family relationships in the genesis and repetition of delinquency is suggested in several studies. In a study conducted by Craig and Gick (1963) found that three factors are to be related to increase the likelihood of delinquency in boys:

1. Careless or inadequate supervision by mother or substitute.
2. Erratic or over strict discipline.
3. Lack of cohesiveness of the family unit.

Similar findings came up in a study conducted by Bandura and Walters (1959) of 26 delinquent's boys and an equal number of no delinquents from the same social class and I.Q. range.

Environment Outside the Home

There are three factors that lie outside the home which may provide the child to fall in the vicious circle of delinquents:

(i) *Bad Companions:* Rejected children from the family fell easily in the company of delinquents as they are accepted there and get recognition and importance in that group. Children of the same age join and carry on the order of the senior delinquents. They are criminals also who induce and exploit the juvenile mind for the act of delinquency.

(ii) *Leisure Time Factor:* Ample of leisure time becomes an important factor for delinquency. It is time to say here that empty mind is a devil's workshop. Now-a-days there are excessive facilities where children can pass their leisure time and develop their personality positively but at the same time there are activities which may lead a child to delinquent acts such as seeing cinema habitually or gambling.

(iii) *Uncongenial Environment of the School:* The uncongenial atmosphere of the school provides mental and moral harms. The child develops and hatred for the school if his class fellows or his leader's behaviour is not congenial. Poor infrastructure of the school becomes one of the factors to develop truancy among the students. Teachers who are very strict also develop hatred for the school among children. To avoid such atmosphere, they go away from the school pass their time with the company of the gangsters and they themselves become delinquents.

Psychological Factors

There are some personal factors which grow out of psychological situations. Such situations and aroused out to disintegration of personality. There factors are:

(i) Feeling of insecurity and revenge.
(ii) Constant frustration.
(iii) Emotional immaturity.
(iv) Getting recognition in the company of anti-social elements.
(v) Poor will power.
(vi) Inferior complex.
(vii) Non-fulfillment of basic, social and psychological desires viz. *(a)* organic, *(b)* personal, and *(c)* social.

In brief it may be stated that heredity as well as environment are responsible for children leading into delinquency. Following lines reveal the true picture; 'Biological and social factors make up the personality but if these factors fail to integrate conflicts lead to repression and various types of delinquencies.'

Treatment of Juvenile Delinquents

It is necessary to solve the problems of the delinquent children. The co-operation of parents, government, school, psychologists, and others who are doing community work, is required as problem cannot be solved by one agency only. It is pertinent here to say, 'prevention is better than cure'. However if one wants to prevent a child to be delinquent, one should provide the facilities or environment where all the biological, psychological and social needs of the child should completely be fulfilled without fail.

Following steps may be taken into consideration to treat the delinquent children.

Social Treatment Method

In this method attempt is made to modify and reform the social environment with the intention to the fulfillment of needs of the child especially psychological needs. Some of the significant points should be kept in mind while dealing delinquent children by the parents and teachers.

1. Parents and children should never be blamed for their delinquent behaviour.
2. Parents should be guided and encouraged to express freely regarding the delinquent behaviour of the child.
3. Bulk of suggestions to the parents should be avoided.
4. One or two suggestions at a time should be given to parents.
5. Delinquent children must be encouraged to express their needs or give out whatever in their minds.
6. They should be provided some responsibility which will bring proper development of their personality.

Treatment of the Delinquents by the Parents in the Home

1. Parents should express interest, positive attitude and sympathy with the delinquent child.
2. Love and affection will be helpful in removing the delinquency in the child not strictness.
3. Cruelty, scolding and rebuking to the delinquent child should not be practised at all.
4. Proper environment to each child should be created where he can express his views without any hesitation.
5. He should be kept at an arm's length with the members of the family who exercise a bad influence on him.

6. The immoral and improper behaviour of other family members should be discouraged and if possible it should be stopped earliest.
7. The attitude of parents toward sex should psychological and proper.
8. Parents should make arrangements to provide sex education if they cannot give it to their child.
9. Avoid family misunderstanding.

Treatment of the Delinquents in the School by the Teacher

The teacher plays a significant and important role in the development of the child's personality. He is capable to prevent children not to involve in delinquent activities and also cure them if any child has already in such activities. The teacher may treat them by adopting the following treatments:

1. The delinquent child should be removed from that school and sent over to the other one.
2. The teacher should be sympathetic with the delinquent children instead to ignoring them.
3. The teacher should assign more constructive and activities keeping in view his ability and capability.
4. The teacher should establish rapport with the delinquent child to find out the real cause of his misbehaviour.
5. The teacher may sublimate his frustration especially sex by providing him opportunities such as to play drama, dance, composition of poems learning music etc.
6. Classroom discipline should be democratic and create such an atmosphere in the class, where other children may have faith to the delinquent children. Self-concept should be developed in the child.
7. Self-regarding sentiment and self-concept should be developed properly.

Treatment of the Delinquents by the Psychologists and Psycho-analysts

Nothing is more important than the psychological clinic for the treatment of delinquents. Cyril Burt has suggested, 'for successful treatment and prevention of juvenile delinquency, there is one measure which seems to be essential as it is definite the establishment of psychological clinic.

According to psycho-analysts, the behavioural action of the delinquents is caused due to the repressed desires or wishes lying in the unconscious mind. Freud rightly said, 'there can be no adult neurosis without infantile neurosis'. It indicates that while treating delinquents, psycho-analysts shall have looked back to the experiences of the infant and their repressed desires that are lying in their unconscious. In this regard, there are two methods which are generally employed:

1. Free Association Methods.
2. Dream Analysis Methods.

Psychological methods which are employed to treat the delinquent children are:

(a) *Psycho Drama:* In this method, the plot is selected according to the problem of the delinquent who is to act the role of a character in a natural and spontaneous manner. A psychologist studies the drama and asks the questions while the acting is going on and at last he pacifies the emotional reactions.

(b) *Non-directive Technique:* This technique is based on the principle that every delinquent is capable to solve his or her problem. This technique has the following four aspects:

   1. Psycho-analyst allows the delinquent to express his/her emotions freely. He is to listen the client attentively and patiently.
   2. Noting is done by the psychologist. He reflects the emotions of the client like a mirror.
   3. The attitude of the psychologist is very positive as well as democratic.
   4. No decision or opinion on the ideas and thoughts of the delinquent is given by the psychologist. As no direction is given by the psychologist so it is known as the non-directive technique.

Steps Taken by the Government Agencies to Treat Juvenile Delinquents

The government adopts the following methods to reform delinquents:

1. *Juvenile Courts*: These type of courts are meant to search out the causes of offences in a psychological manner and provide justice to them. The following are taken:

   (a) Warning is issued and they sent free.
   (b) They are freed under the strict supervision of parents or the guardians.

(c) They are released on probation. Sometimes they are freed under the supervision of some responsible person if parents are not considered suitable by the court.

2. *Probation Officer:* If the behaviour of the delinquent is very problematic, the court puts up him under the charge of probation officer whose job is to reform the delinquents.
3. *Reformations:* Reformations have been arranged for the treatment of delinquents. In such reformatories there is arrangements for reading, writing, recreation and there is also provision to train them to do occupational and vocational job as it is based on the principle, 'poverty is the main cause of delinquency.'
4. *Borstal Institution:* In such institution strict discipline like jail is maintained but delinquents are provided the best possible education.

Prevention of Delinquent Behaviour of Children

It is true that 'prevention is better than cure.' As mentioned earlier that there are various causes of delinquency, parents and teachers must create such as environment where most of their psychological and social needs may be fulfilled. However, following procedure should be adopted to prevent delinquency.

1. Parents should provide all possible facilities to their offspring. They should handle them psychologically and provide very congenial atmosphere to develop personality positively. Clifford's words may be quoted here, 'a satisfying family life protects against delinquency.'
2. *Recreation:* It is a general tendency among the children to play. It is the play through which the child expresses all his frustrations, tensions and anxieties therefore parents/teachers should provide proper arrangements for recreations.
3. *Child Guidance Clinics:* Parents/teachers should have vigil if any delinquent behaviour comes up. He should immediately be referred to the guidance clinic where he should be brought to the right direction.
4. *Proper Education:* Undoubtedly education plays a vital role in preventing delinquency among children. Moral education should be given from the very beginning in the school as well as in the family.

5. *Curriculum of the Education:* Proper syllabus is very important as it can lead to proper utilization of the mental and physical energy. It should have the following content in the curriculum:
   (a) Each unit of the subject like literature should have some elements of moral ethical and value education.
   (b) Attention should be given on creative activity.
   (c) Co-curricular activities should be incorporated in the curriculum.
   (d) Proper utilization of leisure time.

QUESTIONS

A. Long Answer Type Questions

1. Define 'Juvenile Delinquency'. Evaluate critically its different causes. Suggest some preventive measure.
2. Who is delinquent? Discuss Various methods of identifying them.
3. 'Poverty is the main cause of delinquency.' Discuss.
4. Discuss various characteristics, needs and problems of the delinquents. Suggest plan for their education.

B. Short Answer Type Questions

1. Discuss programme for educating delinquents.
2. Discuss the role of teachers and parents in treatment of delinquents.
3. Discuss psychological causes of juvenile delinquency.
4. 'Delinquents are not born but made.' Comment.

C. Objective Type Questions

1. Enrichment triad programme is more popular to correct delinquents. True/false
2. Delinquents are:
   1. Academically Superior 2. Emotionally Unstable
   3. Poor Adjustment in Home and School.
   (a) 1 and 2 are correct (b) 2 and 3 are correct
   (c) 1 and 3 are correct (d) 1, 2 and 3 are correct
3. Delinquent children have positive self-concept. True/false.

SUGGESTED READINGS

1. Burt, C., *The Young Delinquent*, University of London Press Ltd., St. Hugh's School Beckely.
2. Shanker, Uday (1959). *Problem Children*, Atma Ram and Sons, Delhi.
3. Hurlock, Elizabeth B. (1969). *Adolescent Development*, McGraw Hill Book Company N.Y.
4. Mussen, Paul H. and Others (1969). *Child Development and Personality*. (3rd edn.) Harper and Row.

11

Mental Retardation

Mental deficiency is a condition of subnormal mental development present at birth or early childhood. Mental retardation is a term generally used by psychiatrists educational and clinical psychologists and characterized by limited intelligence and social inadequacy. Commonly used terms that are synonymous with 'mental deficiency' are feeble mindedness, amentia and olgophrenia. It has been shown that the distribution of intelligence in the general population is bell shaped. In any large selected group of children, there will be a considerable number who have I Q's below 90 and an equal number with IQ's above 110. As we go down the scale from 90 IQ and up the scale from 110 IQ, the number of cases gradually decreases. There are children who possess sub-average intellectual functioning or suffer from mental retardation on one account or the other. These children show retardation in acquiring intellectual competence, emotional stability and social maturity. Although they are physically grown-up they show such emotional and social behaviours which are appropriate to children of much lower age.

Mental retardation is stated as a significantly below average level of intelligence measured by an individually administered intelligence test. In mental retardation, a person's social as well as intellectual functioning must be impaired.

A DSM-IV diagnosis of mental retardation is indicated when there are deficits in at least two of the following skill areas:

1. Communication.
2. Self care.
3. Home living.

4. Social and interpersonnal skills.
5. Use of community resources.
6. Self-direction.
7. Functional academic skills.
8. Work health, leisure and safety.

Mental retardation is regarded as a chromic, irreversible condition that begins before the age of 18. If intellectual functioning drops to retarded level after age 18, the problem is classified as a dementia rather than mental retardation. The basic learning processes of most mental retardates aside from a minority with serious neurological defects are not essentially different from these of normal children. The problem which the retardation typically encounters in learning basic academic skills may be summarized according to James C. Coleman as follows:

1. *Difficulty in Focusing Attention :* The retardates poor learning is often due to the fact that his attention is focused on irrelevant aspects of learning situation.
2. *Deficiency in Past Learning:* Most formal learning requires prior learning *e.g.* A child on entering school will fall farther and farther behind if he has not previously learned basic verbal, conceptual and problem solving skills.
3. *Expectancy of Failure – A Self-Fulfilling Prophecy:* Because of having experience more failure in learning attempts than other children, the mentally retarded child tends to begin tasks with a greater expectancy of failure and to engage in avoidance behaviour as well. Thus, if he gets success in a task, he may not perceive his success as due to his own efforts or ability.

These learning difficulties are not exclusive to retardation but they are common among them.

Definition

'Mental retardation' according to the American Association on Mental Deficiency (AAMD) is "subaverage intellectual functioning which originates during the developmental period and is associated with impairment in *adaptive behaviour*" (Helber, 1961). The inclusion of the word adaptive is important here as it helps to take cultural setting into account—an individual capable of adaptive behaviour in rural setting might experience greater difficulties in urban settings.

The AAMD has given the comprehensive definition. But it has been revised in 1983, H.J. Grossman defined mental retardation as follows.

"Mental retardation refers to significantly subaverage general intellectual functioning existing concurrently with deficit in adaptive behaviour and manifested during the developmental period."

Here *'significantly subaverage'* refers to I.Q. approximately below 70.

'Adaptive behaviour' relates to the degree or extent with which the individual can meet the standard of personal as well as social responsibility which are expected for his/her age and cultural group, and

'Development period' refers to ages between birth and eighteen years.

Thus low intellectual functioning and inability to adopt to the demands of society may be considered as adequate definition of mental retardation.

Labels of Mental Retardation

It has generally been agreed that there are three levels of retardation, which have been distinguished; only the labels have varied according to time and setting. The terms moron, imbecile, and idiot, were once acceptable designations for retarded individuals. Today the AAMD uses the term mild moderate and severe and profound to refer to substantially the same categories.

Current labels used by educators reflect more completely the school capabilities of each group, here we find that educable (EMR), trainable (TMR) and custodial levels of retardation are distinguished. The following Table 11.1 shows the parallels alongwith the generally accepted range for each category.

Table-11.1

Terminology Used to Describe the Mentally Retarded

I.Q. Range	*50-60/70*	*25-49*	*Below 25*
Early Labelling	Moron	Imbecile	Idiot
AAMD and WHO	Mild	Moderate	Severe profound
Current Educational Labelling	Educable	Trainable	Custodial

Current Characteristics of Mentally Retarded Children

1. Mentally retarded children are slow to walk, talk and feed themselves.
2. They take unusually long period of time before they are toilet-trained.
3. In the more severe cases, retardation extends to almost all areas of development.
4. Retarded individuals have IQs that range from below 25 to 60 or 70.
5. The longest group of retarded individual have IQs that range from 50 to 60 or 70, classified as mildly moron or educably mentally retarded they are rarely institutionalized. Such type of a mentally retarded child will have a difficult time in school and is likely to lag behind intellectually average children of the same age.
6. An educably retarded youngster can acquire many of the academic skills mastered by elementary school children but reaches this level of achievement at a later age.
7. The moderately or trainable retarded with IQs ranging from 25 to 49 usually unable to hold jobs except within sheltered workshops, they rarely marry and usually are institutionalized.
8. Mentally retarded are incapable of adequate self-care, self-support or self-management in society.
9. Such children have little control over their impulses. Their sense of right and wrong is poorly developed.
10. Biological drives are well-developed at the intermediate level but the affective aspect is mainly limited to the simpler emotions of pleasure, fear, anger and surprise.
11. Mentally retarded individuals rarely experience sentiments involving honour, social righteousness and duty.
12. Mentally retarded children are suggestive and easily be influenced. They tend to be submissive.
13. Some times they are either stable, apathetic or unstable and excitable.
14. Defective speech and shuffling gait are two very prominent characteristics of these individuals.
15. They are relatively insensitive to pain and their auditory and visual defects are common.

Classification of Mental Retardation According to Degree of Deficiency

The feeble minded or mentally retarded children are classified as: (1) Idiots, (2) Imbeciles and (3) Moron. This classification was issued by Doll, E.A. (1930). This is the gradation from one level to the next is continuous.

1. *Idiocy or Idiots*

It is the lowest level of mental deficiency. They have IQs under 20 and their maximum level of mental or social development is less than three years. Even as adults, they must be cared for as if they were infants. They need help in dressing, washing and eating and must be protected against common physical dangers. Language is limited to a simple words or grunts.

2. *Imbecility or Imbeciles*

It is an intermediate state. They have IQ's from 20 to 50. They may attain mental ages ranging from three to seven and a half years. They can be taught to care for their simple bodily needs and to protect themselves against common physical danger. They are incapable of profiting from ordinary school work. If physically well developed they may be trained to run errands, sweep floors, feed animals and do simple weeding. They are unable to earn their own living and must be closely supervised as well as supported.

3. *Moronity or Moron*

It is the highest grade of mental deficiency. Their mental age may range from seven and a half to ten and a half years. Their I.Q. ranges from 50 to 60. Persons having I.Q. 70 may also be diagnosed as mental defectives. However their deciding point is their social maturity. When properly taught they can learn 3 R's. They rarely attain scholastic achievements beyond the fourth grade level. Under favourable conditions they are capable of earning a living or atleast contributing to their support.

The Six Hours Retarded Child

It is a concept which states that students who perform poorly in school may function adequately at home and within community. Such children are not considered as retarded.

This concept has come up in the late 1980s. Today most of the psychologist and educationists have accepted that children identified as mildly retarded educable during their school age years manifest retarded are functioning well outside the school. Edgerton (1984) suggests that regular and special education programmes should prepare children with limited potential for the roles they would play as adults.

Classification of Mental Retardation According to the Rate of Educability

There are different ways to classify retarded children, the method generally favoured by educators is to classify such children by their expected level of educational progress. Educationists have divided them into three group as mentioned in the Table 11.1.

1. ***Educable Mentally Retarded (EMR) Children***

(I.Q. 50 to 75) are normal in appearance but they are said to function at an intellectual level generally limited to learning only the most basic school skills in reading, spelling, writing and numerical calculation. Most of the such children begin school in the regular classroom, but low achievement or adaptive behaviour makes it necessary for many to receive special assistance or attend special classes. During pre-school years, they develop some social and communication skills although there is some lag in developing sensory and motor functioning but with parental assistance and special training, they can be taught to be self-supporting. It has been found that their out of school success usually depends more on social skills than on occupational ones. Thus parents of these children must avoid the temptation to foster dependency, sloppiness and other social undesirable characteristics, 'excusing' them because of intellectual deficit.

2. ***Trainable Mentally Retarded (TMR) Children***

(I.Q. 30 to 50) function at a level where formal academic learning is quite limited. Most of such children can be expected to have physical or sensory impairments and many tend to look different in terms of facial features or physical characteristics. TMR children emerge quite early in infancy or pre-school years. Generally they are placed in special class or in special schools; they need training in self-care activities and language development. They only acquire, in many cases rudimentary academic skills.

3. ***Profoundly Mentally Retarded Children***

I.Q. below 30 are for the most part totally dependent on others for their existence and many are institutionalized early in life. Quality of education and treatment of such children, behaviour modification and environmental stimulation techniques are to be used as much as possible to enable them to achieve some level of independence within supervised environments.

Classification on the Basis of Degree of Retardation

We also use the terms mildly retarded and severely retarded instead of educable and trainable, because they connote degrees of difference rather than clear cut educational distinctions.

Levels of Mental Retardation: (According to AAM D)

1. *Mildly Mentally Retarded Individual* (I.Q. 55-70)

Mildly retarded children constitute the largest portion of the mentally retarded population. They tend to be slow lacking in alertness, curiosity and spontaneity of emotional reactions. They are easily befooled, credulous and easily led into anti-social or criminal acts or other forms of undesirable behaviour. They are usually not identified before reaching school age. Although such children may have problems in communication, physical development and socialization during the pre school years.

2. *Moderate Mental Retardation* (I.Q. 40-54)

Such children can learn some communication skills by the age of 5 or 6 years although they cannot freely mix with others in the society. Their motor development is shown than normal children but most of them can adapt to home life with some training. They can wash, dress feed themselves and use the toilet. But they are incapable of learning in ordinary schools, very few untreated PKU victims have I.Q. above 50, if treatment, which involves a restrictive diet, is started early most of these changes can be prevented, although earlier damage can not be reversed. They usually appear to be cleansy and dirty in their dresses. Mostly they suffer from badly deformities and poor motor co-ordination. Such children are found to be hostile and aggressive through typically they appear simple looking.

3. *Severe Mental Retardation* (I.Q. 25-39)

The severe mental retardation shows at the age of 3 to 5 years poor motor as well as language development. If they are provided training, they can learn though very slowly, to communicate with other by signs and simple language and take care of their personal needs. Such children are identified before reaching school age. Many at higher functioning levels may be able to achieve some measure of economic self-sufficiency, but this often in a sheltered workshop but have continuing difficulties in social adjustment.

4. Profoundly Mentally Retarded Individuals (I.Q. below 25)

These children have generally special needs for continuous supervision or custodial care. Such children may have to be placed in residential facilities as they grow older. It is most serious of all. They show very little sensory-motor and language development.

Etiology

It must be kept in mind before discussing etiology that mental retardation is merely a symptom- not a disease. It is evident that mental retardation results most likely from the complex interplay of familial, environmental and social factors in which heredity tends to set limits on intellectual potential or capacity whereas experience determines to what extent such potential will be fulfilled. There are the following types of causes associated with mental retardation.

1. Familial

It includes the small percentage of each ethnic group that falls at the lower end of the polygenetic distribution of intelligence for their respective groups. A familial retarded child may be viewed as having an I.Q. within the lower range of the normal distribution. Most children in this category are only mildly retarded with I.Qs ranging from 50 to 69 sometimes it is 85. They are physically normal and have no history of brain damage or neurological defects.

2. Biological Caused of Mental Retardation

It is caused by some particular biological damage or defect. These include chromosomal anomalies such as:

(i) *Mongolism (Down's Syndromic):* It is caused by chromosomal aberration. This is a condition caused by the presence of an extra chromosome. It has been revealed that in Down's Syndrome there are forty-seven chromosomes instead of the usual forty six and that chromosome pair number twenty-one is not a pair but in a triplet or trisomy condition. Children with Down Syndrome have a 99 per cent chance of being retarded. There is a considerable variability in the level of retardation, which may range from mild to severe. In general such children are especially weak in tactile perception, higher level abstraction and reasoning and auditory perception. The number of physical features are often found among children who suffer from this symptom. They have slanting eyes, flat face and nose, large and deeply fissured tongue, irregular and misshapen teeth etc. Their height as an adult does not exceed four feet. Mongoloid children perform better in a family where there is emotional warmth rather than in institutions. With proper guidance and encouragement, they can perform simple household work.

(ii) *Microcephaly (Small Headedness):* It refers to an arrest in the development of the brain at the fourth or fifth month of foetal life. The cause of this defect is the impaired development of the brain and a consequent failure of the cranium to attain normal size.

(iii) *Hydrocephaly :* The accumulation of an abnormal amount of cerebrospinal fluid within the cranium causes damage to the brain tissues and the enlargement of the cranium. It accounts the causes of paralysis of limbs and leg is a prominent symptom.

(iv) *Phenylketonuria (PKU):* It is an inherited metabolic disorder in which the body is unable to oxidize the chemical phenylalanuine, which therefore accumulate in the body, if it is allowed to continue, severe mental retardation may result.

(v) *Cretinism (Thyroid Deficiency):* Thyroid gland is located in the lower portion of the neck region. It produces hormone *i.e.* thyroxine. This controls basal metallic rate. Early deprivation of thyroxine leads to cretinism or a type of feeble mindedness. Thyroid deficiency in adulthood leads to a condition referred to as myxodema which is characterized by overweight and general sluggishness. Thyroid deficiency is due to a relative absence of iodine in the diet of the child. Cretins are malformed dwarfs with a bloated appearance. The brain like other tissues fail to develop normally.

(vi) *Congenital Syphilis:* Children born to syphilitic mothers are sometimes infected with the disease through the placental circulation while still in utero. Most of such cases terminate in abortion or are born dead. Of those born alive, a large proportion show normal mental development, but other are retarded or feeble minded. Most mental defectives with congenital syphilis are idiots or imbeciles.

Table–11.2
Biological Cause of Mental Retardation

Type of Event	*Example*
1. Systematic disease	Down's syndrome, PKU, Cretinism
2. Infectious disease	Rubella/Germany Measles, Encephatities, Syphilis
3. Physical trauma	Malnutrition, Poisoning, Hypoxia/ Oxygen deprivation

3. *Problems During Pre-natal Period*

If the expectant mother suffers from several malnutrition or any severe infectious disease, the growth of the foetus is likely to be affected. Toxic substance like cigarettes, alcohol consumption or certain drugs can also cause mental retardation in the foetus.

Pre-natal Causes

Occurring before birth these causes can be genetic or environmental. The most common example of a genetic cause of all cases of severe retardation is the chromosomal disorder known as Down's Syndrome and phenyl ketonuria which have already been discussed earlier.

4. *Perinatal Environmental Causes*

Maternal infections such as rubella (German measles) or CMV (Megalia Virus) a common virus similar to chickenpox can cross the placental barrier and attack the foetus, if any symptoms in the mother. It is essential that expectant mothers be vaccinated against such viruses.

5. *Post-natal Factors*

These occur after birth and are associated with a number of childhood diseases such as encephalites or meningitis in which sustained high fever especially during the first two years of life may result damage to the developing brain. Other factors such as asphyxia, a blow to the head, accidents with neurological complications can alter intellectual development and result in severe mental retardation.

6. *Nutritional*

The chronic malnutrition either in the mother or sub sequently in the developing child, may be one of the more significant factors in eventual mental performance. A lack of sufficient nutrients during critical periods of brain growth often results in mild retardation.

Home and Educational Environment

It is very true that a child's home environment plays a primary role in all aspects of social and emotional development. It is not surprising to state that some distinct pattern of home and family environment accompany retardation. The family factors which are related to retardation include low achievement motivation of the parents, father's absence, lack of appropriate sex role models, impoverished financial status and low emphasis on education. A rather important role that early home experiences may play in retardation has to do with the child's motivation. Retarded children may have more frequently been neglected by adults in their early lives and therefore crave attention and praise to a greater degree than their mental age alone would predict.

All education is based on incentives of one sort or another, but it has been suggested that retarded children may be motivated by different incentives that are the typical middle class youngsters whose needs determine, so many of our educational practices. Children who lack sufficient environmental stimulation during critical periods of infancy and early childhood usually fail to develop at the normal rate children from low SES, lack of sufficient sensory stimulation, perceptual experience, adequate adult language models and a variety of other experiences necessary for cognitive growth and development. The familial, biological nutritional and environment causes are not mutually exclusive. They are meant that underly the very complex syndrome of mild retardation. It is true that SES variables have more than just a correlational relationship with mild retardation. It is also evident that a very large number of children in this group come from families of low socio-economic status. Because in many cases their parents I.Qs also fall in the mildly retarded range. It can be put in this way to solve the role of heredity and environment in the mental growth and development. Heredity provides a range of possibilities for the developing child but the child's level of achievement within that rather wide range might be attributable to the environments in which he or she grows up.

Treatment and Educational Provisions

Mildly Retarded Children/Educationable/Moron

The most common form of education for the children having I.Qs 50 to 70 has been the special education class room but the approach has been replaced by programmes that include as much integration in regular classroom as possible special education classes at the primary level (ages 6 to 8) provide experiences in oral language and speech development, sensori-motor development, self-awareness, group membership and social adjustment. Academic tasks are not emphasized except for beginning instruction in counting and recognition of letters or words.

By elementary level (ages 8 to 13) such children have begun to learn tool-skill subjects such as reading writing spelling and maths units in basic social studies and practical science are also taught and the activities in which tool-skill subjects can be applied and practiced.

The secondary programme provides consolidation in the use of basic academic skills learned earlier but stress is given on preparation for work and home living.

Special education for mildly retarded children, whether in main streamed or special classroom environment would continue to focus on

(i) developing basic academic skills.
(ii) special competence.
(iii) personal adjustment.
(iv) occupational adequacy.

Approaches to education for them stress the need for two basic skill that cut across all curriculum areas.

1. Thinking critically or being able to weigh the facts of a given situation together with their implications and
2. Acting independently or making a decision based on these facts and following it through:

Mentally retarded children do not outgrow their mental retardation as they reach maturity. No amount of training or medical care will transform a mentally defective child into a normal child. As described above with suitable training and guidance, the majority of retarded children who belong to this category (moron) educable or mildly retarded) are capable of some degree of profitable employment and social self-management. The first step to be taken in the treatment of the mental defective is to:

1. *Parent Education:* Educate parents to accept the child's limitations and the permanency of his/her mental defect. Their false belief is to be eradicated from the mind that with special educational training and medical attention he can be made normal.
2. *Home Training:* The home is the natural place for the beginning of training since almost all mental defectives live their own homes during infancy and the great majority continue to live in even as adults. Most of such children require much time and patience, of major importance is the emotional attitude of the mother. There are mothers who reject and ignore their defective off spring and others are over protective to the point of depriving the healthy siblings in the family of their share of her attention and affection. As the child grows up, he should be assigned responsibilities and duties that are within his mental limits. Misdeeds and temper outbursts should be checked and every attempt made to develop a pleasant disposition.
3. *School Training:* It is often desirable to postpone sending such children to school until they are about eight since 6 year old moron has a mental age of three to four year's . The class may proceed at a slow pace with more emphasis on developing motor-co-ordination, speech and desirable social traits than on learning abstract and often incomprehensible school subjects.

Mildly retarded slow learner children have been main streamed or integrated into regular classes.

Vocational and Social Skills Training

Knowledge and use of appropriate vocational and social skills are key factors in success both in competitive job environments. Skills training through modelling has been found to be a very effective technique. Group homes, in addition to it are a place where retarded adolescents and adult learn valuable home making and self-management skills. There are several problem situations which can be modelled so that prospective worker may learn to identify both problem behaviours and appropriate ways of dealing with such situations.

Another important aspect of retarded people's lives is a supportive network of people. One way to increase the amount of support available is to help the individual to learn social skills. We know that moron children are very suggestive, due to this characteristics they are vulnerable to personal sexual and financial exploitation. One source of this problem is their tendency to answer 'yes' to all questions regardless of context. One way to prevent exploitation is to pay special attention to teach them what is expected of a person and how to say 'no'.

Main Streaming

It is the integration of mentally retarded children into regular classroom settings. In other words, we may state that the administrative practice of placing exceptional children in regular classroom setting with the support of special education services. Its purpose is to help to make life as normal as possible for the retarded child. In main streaming :

1. Children are assigned to a regular class for atleast half of their school day.
2. Regular classroom procedures are modified only when necessary.
3. Finally, each child's educational needs are assessed on the basis of actual performance in the classroom rather than on the basis of arbitrarily assigned labels.

Teaching Students with Mild Retardation

1. Determine readiness.
2. State and present objectives simply.
3. Base specific learning objectives an on analysis of the child's learning strengths and weaknesses.
4. Present material in small, logical steps.
5. Work on practical skills.
6. Do not skip steps.
7. Be prepared to present the same idea in many different ways.
8. Go back to a simpler level if you see the student is not following.
9. Be especially careful to motivate the student and maintain attention.
10. Be aware that student with retardation must over learn, repeat, and practice more than children of average intelligence.
11. Pay close attention to social relations.

Encouraging Mental Retarded Children for Language Development

1. Talk about things that interest children.
2. Follow the children's lead. Reply to their imitations and comments.
3. Share their excitement.
4. Do not ask too many questions.
5. Encourage children to asks questions.
6. Use pleasant tone of voice.
7. Do not be judgemental or make fun of children's language.
8. Be light and humorous.
9. Allow enough time for children to respond.
10. Treat children with courtesy by not interpreting when they are talking.
11. Encourage participation and listen to their ideas.
12. Provide opportunity for children to use language.

Treatment and Educational Provisions for Severely Mentally Retarded Children (I.Q. 25-39)

Severely mentally retarded in most cases can gain from systematic training in dressing, feeding and toileting. Nursery schools or day care centres, should be established in greater numbers to provide habit training and language development programmes for young children. Special co-operative approaches should also be developed wherein families are trained to assist in their retarded child's development, it is an important that these programmes assist in strengthening the parent child relationship, public education facilites must necessarily be available for severely mentally retarded children of school age. Emphasis should generally be given on (1) language development, (2) Self-help skills, (3) Socialization and (4) preparation, for living and working in sheltered environment.

School activities include practice in listening, following directions, communicating with others, reading or recognizing common signs and labels counting and telling time. Self-help activities should include lessons in dressing grooming, eating, care of personal belongings, toileting and safety. They should also be engaged in arts and crafts, motor and recreational activities, some vocational experiences and practice in home living.

Profoundly Mentally Retarded Individuals (I.Q. below 25)

The profoundly mentally retarded fall at the lower end of severe category have multi handicapping conditions—tend to present unique problems in medical and behavioural management. These children generally have special needs for continuing supervision or custodial care. It is suggested that their educational goals should stress skills that will maximise their happiness within the environment rather than unrealistic expectations for a future role in everyday society.

Table–11.3
AAMD Classification of Mental Retardation with Special Education Categories

AAMD Level	*I.Q. Range*	*Special Education Category*	*Expected Adaptive Behaviour*	*Adult Outcomes*
Mild	50-70	Educable, capable of 2nd to 7th grade learning, such s reading stories, communicating in writing and handling simple financial transaction.	May be responsible for all feeding and personal grooming activities communicate, effectively in every conversation.	Able to live independently, may have children and hold unskilled or semi-skilled jobs.
Moderate	40-54	Trainable or educable capable of first and second grade learning such as reading simple sentences and basic addition and subtraction.	May be able to feed, dress and groom self-care on simple conversations, interact with others.	Able to live independently but will need periodic supervision, can work in sheltered situations.
Severe	25-39	Trainable-capable of some skills at kindergarten level, such as recognizing words and basic number concepts.	Able to feed, toilet and dress well carry on rudimentary conversation and run errands or simple household cares	Will need to live in closely supervised environment
Profound	Below 25	Profound capable of some pre-school activities.	Able to feed self and to interact with others in simple play activities but speech and toileting remain at primilive level.	Will require continued custodial care.

AAMD—The American Association of Mental Deficiency.

Most profoundly retarded persons may have to be placed in residential facilities as they grow older.

QUESTIONS

A. Long Answer Type Questions

1. Discuss the concept of mental retardation and describe its various characteristics.
2. What are the basis of classifying the mentally retarded children? Explain briefly.
3. Discuss the various factors which cause mental retardation.
4. Describe the various education provisions for mentally retarded children.
5. Discuss the general characteristics of mentally retarded children.

B. Short Answer Type Questions

1. Define mental retardation.
2. Discuss the concept of the six hours retarded child.
3. Discuss the provisions for educable mentally handicapped children.
4. Causes of mental retardation.
5. Who is mentally handicapped?

C. Objective Type Questions

1. Mentally retarded child has the I.Q. of
   (*a*) 120 (*b*) 90
   (*c*) 70 (*d*) 110
2. Which is the most important personality characteristics of mentally retarded children.
   (*a*) Bright (*b*) Active
   (*c*) Independent (*d*) Very slow
3. Who is not helpful to be mentally retarded child.
   (*a*) Psychologist (*b*) Rilualist
   (*c*) Psychiatrist (*d*) Counsellor
4. Match List I with List II

	List I	*List II*
(*a*)	Poor performance in school not at home	Idiot
(*b*)	TMR	Cretinism
(*c*)	Lowest level of mental deficiency	6 Hours mental retarded
(*d*)	Hypothyroxine	I.Q. 30 to 50

SUGGESTIVE READINGS

1. Allen, Gorden, 'Patterns of Discovery in the Genetics of Mental Deficiency' *American Journal of Mental Deficiency,* 62, March 1958, pp. 840-49.
2. Biswas, M. (1980). *Mentally Retarded and Normal Children,* New Delhi, Sterling Publisher Pvt. Ltd.
3. Hewett, F.M. (1984). *Educations of Exceptional Learners* (3rd ed.) Allyn and Bacon, Inc.
4. Page, J.D. (1976). *Abnormal Psychology,* Tata McGraw Hill Publishing Co. Ltd.
5. Rao, D.B. (2003). *Problems of Mentally Handicapped Children.* Discovery Publishing House, New Delhi.

12

Gifted Children

'Full many a flower is born to blush unseen,
And waste its sweetness in the desert air.'

—Gray

These lines are aptly applicable to gifted children. If we neglect the gifted children of our nation, we may find ourselves to have a nation with hundred well-trained legs but without a head that would not make effective the work of those legs. It is evident on the basis of studies-conducted in different countries that much of the nation's human resource material of high ability is being wasted. This is because, it is not being adequately identified and developed through proper providing educational facilities and opportunities to the gifted children. It was J.P. Guilford who suggested that understanding human intellectual gifts can help human control to their destiny and happiness. He stated that some individuals are exceptional in traditionally defined ways, such as those measurable by high I.Q. score, other individuals, however, may be exceptional in untraditional ways.

Earlier the concept of gifted was considered to have scores on a standardized I.Q. test and more or less it was also conceived by L.M. Terman in 1925. It had continued to dominate this understanding of giftedness. Actually the gifted individuals represent one end of the continuum of intelligent and talent behaviour. But exceptional ability is not limited to cognitive skills. Some children and adults are exceptional athletes or artists. There are individuals who excel in a particular area far beyond normal expectations but in other areas are rather average. Many gifted artists, pianiosts, and dancers would have only average scores on standardized I.Q. tests The uniqueness of the gifted child enhances rather than handicaps. It is positive than a negative characteristics that facilitates rather than restricts.

Definition, Meaning and Concept of Giftedness

Paul Witty defines,' gifted children are those whose performance in a worthwhile endeavour is consistently remarkable as well as those who are academically superior.'

Having Hurst, R.J. says, 'gifted children are those individuals who from kindergarten through high school age show unusual promises in some socially useful and whose talent might be stimulated.'

Hollingsworth defined, 'by a gifted child we mean one who is far more educable than generally the children are:

According to Gallagher, 'the ability to manipulate internally learned symbol systems is perhaps the *sine qua non* of giftedness. He states that such an ability allows gifted learners to learn on their own to initiate rather than follow, to imagine and to create. He considers, 'gifted learners as those who by virtue of outstanding abilities are capable of high performance in academic areas, creative or productive thinking, leadership, visual and performing arts and psychomotor functioning.'

Lucitio (1963) defined, 'the gifted are those whose potential intellectual powers are at such a high ideational level in both productive and evaluative thinking that it can be reasonably assumed, they could be the future problem solvers, innovators and evaluators of the culture if adequate educational experiences are provided.'

If we analyze the Witty's and Having Hurst's definitions we find that former view states that children's whose I.Q. is above 140 and also have their academic performance is superb, they are gifted while later stresses that every child who is superior in some ability makes an outstanding contribution to the welfare and quality of human being at the international level. It may be stated that the greater educability may consist in surpassing power to achieve literacy and abstract intelligence or may be among the lines of arts as in music or drawing or in the sphere of mechanical or other renowned aptitudes. However, it is the field of educationists and psychologists to consider all forms of giftedness in pupils in reference to how unusual individuals may be trained for their own welfare and that of society at large.

Now it is very clear that since 1950's conceptions and definitions of giftedness have evolved to become more inclusive and far beyond the I. Q.

According to Renzulli, it has served the very useful purpose of calling attention to a wider variety of abilities that should be included in a definition of giftedness. Renzulli's 'Three Ring Conception of Giftedness' is quite break through in that as it gives flavour to whole endeavour of programme for the gifted children. According to it giftedness consists of an interaction among three basic clusters of human traits – these clusters being above average general abilities, high level of task commitment and high level of creativity. Gifted and talented children are those possessing or capable of developing this composite set of traits and applying them to any potentially valuable area of human performance (Renzulli *et al.* 1981).

Tannenbaum's (1983) psychological definition of giftedness broadens our understanding of how different factors other than intellectual, interact, accelerate or inhibit the realization of one's giftedness. These factors include:

- *(a)* General ability, the 'g' factor.
- *(b)* Special ability – special aptitudes and capacities.
- *(c)* Non-intellectual factors – ego strength dedication, willingness to make sacrifices.
- *(d)* Environmental factors home, school and community settings which provide stimulation and support.
- *(e)* Chance factors – unforeseen circumstances in opportunity structure and prevalent life styles which can affect outlets for gifted performances.

A child can attain a gifted level of performance on when he/she is:

1. relatively free of biological impairments.
2. mostly invulnerable to environmental stresses that tend to limit performance (active ego).
3. reared in an environment that supports performance.

Hence, giftedness is the outcome of appropriate enrichment and stimulation of the interaction between unique genetic make up and the environment.

Marland (1972) also reported that gifted and talented children are those who are capable of high performance but may have demonstrated it as high achievement but have potential in any of the following areas singly or in combination:

(a) general intellectual ability.
(b) specific academic aptitude.
(c) creative or productive thinking.
(d) leadership ability.
(e) Affective domain of performing arts.
(f) Psychomotor ability.

Causes of Giftedness

Kitano and Kirby (1986) stated that the giftedness is biologically determined but Gottfried (1984) stressed on individual's socio-economic—status to be associated with his/her giftedness. While Jenson (1969) suggested a midway threshold hypothesis which states that heredity is the basis in setting up the intellectual potential of a person and the environment determines how much of it is realized.

Giftedness has been viewed as resulting from abnormalities, motivational sources, qualitative superiority and quantitative superiority (Anastasi, 1958). Although very high I.Q. children (above 180) may experience 'special perplexities' and puzzling difficulties (Hollingsworth, 1942) related to a lack of friends who can really converse with them Sigmund Freud and other psychologists believed that strong motivational rather than strong intellectual forces were the real determinants of giftedness, certain defence mechanisms such as sublimation and compensation drive individuals with seemingly ordinary minds and talents to achieve gifted accomplishments.

The gifted are qualitatively unlike other human beings, functioning on another plane or in a different world. The gifted and the average are simply at different points along the same line. The differences are due to degree and not to kind. Terman in his study demonstrated that that the gifted are very superior with respect to the same abilities ordinary individuals possess.

As Jenson (1969) concluded that 70 to 85 per cent of intelligence is determined by heredity while Watson (1924) had claimed environmental experience was the potent determiner of intellectual functioning. However, it is stated clearly that interaction between capacity (heredity) and experience (environment) is responsible for an individual's functioning level including his/her intelligence.

Identification of the Gifted Children

Earlier identification of gifted children was left to the classroom teacher but studies suggest that so many children who were not gifted, were selected and that many actually and truly gifted children were overlooked. Teachers stressed on academic and social success with talent in areas such as drama or art tend to promote identification as gifted whereas under achievement, shyness and non-conformity can result in an individual's being excluded from consideration as gifted. Teacher nomination was the only method of identifying gifted children. Gallagher (1975) regarded this method as limited because many children who have high aptitude for reasoning and conceptualization are not performing well in school.

Later on group intelligence and achievement scores, grades, previously demonstrated accomplishments, individual's intelligence test scores and scores tests of creativity were used to identify gifted children. However, teacher observation and nomination was reported to be the major identification procedure of a large number of schools.

Now-a-days we use the following procedures to identify gifted children as it is very difficult to identify giftedness with the help of a single tool or test.

1. Behavioural observation.
2. Teachers' opinions and their ratings.
3. Measurement of I.Q. and creativity.

1. Behavioural Observation

Parents, teachers educationists, psychologists and social workers may be helpful in identifying gifted children at a very early stage on the basis of observation of their Behaviour. There may be so many cues that indicate the giftedness of the children. It is they who play an important role in observing the following cues among gifted children.

(i) curiosity behaviour.
(ii) high ability for symbolic thinking.
(iii) high expressive ability.
(iv) longer span of attention.
(v) self-critical and high aspirations.
(vi) extraordinary memory.
(vii) larger vocabulary for the age level.

Children would not reveal all above identifiable behaviour but are present by and large in the gifted children. Some may be observed more readily in informal settings.

2. *Teachers' Opinions and Ratings*

Teachers are successful only about 10 per cent to 50 per cent of the time in picking out the gifted in their classes (Fox, 1981). The following seven questions, taken from early study of gifted students are still good guides today (Walton, 1961).

1. Who learns easily and rapidly?
2. Who uses a lot of common-sense and practical knowledge?
3. Who retains easily what he/she has heard ?
4. Who knows about many things, that the other children do not know?
5. Who uses large number of words easily and accurately?
6. Who recognizes relations and comprehends meanings?
7. Who is alert and keenly observant and responds quickly? Based on Renzulli and Reis (1991), on their definition of giftedness, it might be added.
8. Who is persistent and highly motivated on some tasks?
9. Who is creative, often has unusual ideas or makes interesting connections.

Renzulli and his associates (1971) suggested a scale which consists of four areas of behaviour through which the teacher can identify giftedness:

A. Learning Characteristics

1. Advanced vocabulary for age and grade level.
2. Independent reading habits prefers advanced level books.
3. Quick mastery and recall of factual information.
4. Ability to make valid generalization.

B. Motivational Characteristics

1. Self starting.
2. Persistence in task completion.
3. Striving for perfection.
4. Bored with routine task.

C. Creative Characteristics

1. Greater curiosity.
2. Greater originality in problem solving.

3. Less concern with conformism.

D. Leadership Characteristics

1. Self-confidence and success with peers.
2. Ready to bear responsibility.
3. Easily adapt to view situations.

Paul Witty (1955) summarized the following areas in his book, *Gifted Children, Our Greatest Resources* in which the accelerated development of gifted children may be identified by parents or members of family before the child enters the school.

(i) Good vocabulary,
(ii) interest in and liking books,
(iii) early interest in calendars, in telling times and in clocks,
(iv) ability to concentrate or to attend longer period than is usual for children,
(v) demonstration of proficiency in drawing, music or other art forms,
(vi) language proficiency, the use of entire sentences and ability to produce a story at an early stage,
(vii) keen observation,
(viii) interest in exploration and discovery of cause-effect relationship,
(ix) the early development of ability to read.

3. Measurement of I.Q. and Creativity

Marland (1972) recommended administering the following tests in order to identify the gifted children:

1. Group intelligence test.
2. Individual intelligence test.
3. Previously demonstrated achievements.
4. Standardized achievement tests.
5. Teacher observation.
6. A case study approach.

It should be remember that students with remarkable abilities in one area may have much less impressive abilities in other areas.

Characteristics of Gifted Children

1. Gifted children are quite socially aware and sensitive (Strang, 1963). If academic achievement is not accorded prestige by their classmates and if superior work on their part puts them

invisible, no valued position with other children, they may actually do poorer work in order to maintain acceptance. Strang also suggested that public praise by the teacher may actually decrease the learning efforts to gifted children, if they sense that it will be detrimental to their relations with classmates.

2. Gifted children tend to prefer those indoor games which are less popular with average children. Terman's study also indicates this fact that children play social games such as chess which is less popular among average children because of the demand on intelligence.
3. Mental health of gifted children has been found consistently superior in relation to mental illness rates within general population. Gallagher (1974) stated that social and emotional problems can and do occur among gifted children. These problems stem from some general sources as those found among disturbed children of average ability. However, since there is a tendency for the high I.Q. child to come from a better family than the average I.Q. child and to possess superior health, the probable occurrence of psychological problems is lessened.
4. Gifted children who belong to high socio-economic–status spent more time in reading during recreational hours and the lower status gifted were more interested in action and competitive team sports (Frierson, 1965).
5. Gifted children from lower class homes experience more family tensions and their performance is lowered than their predicted achievement level.
6. Gifted children are well adjusted in home and in school. They are emotionally stable and self-confident and are well accepted in the class.
7. The language development of gifted children is refined and elaborated.
8. Gifted children display independent and original thinking and high problem solving ability.
9. Gifted children exhibit novelty in their expression and have greater range of interests.

Terman's studies reveal the following characteristics of gifted children:

1. Performance is better in solving specific problems.

2. Greater reasoning ability as expressed while solving problems.
3. Action oriented behaviour.
4. More productive in individual and small group situations.
5. High aspiration for prestigious professions.
6. Display goal oriented behaviour.
7. High perseverance.
8. High analytic perceptual ability.

The gifted children have above average physical development Baldwin conducted body measurement of 594 children of Terman's gifted group having I.Q. ranging from 130 to 189. These children appeared to be physically superior to the comparison group. Terman (1925) found the following physical measures of children:

(i) Greater weight at birth.
(ii) Earlier walking and talking.
(iii) Earlier pubescence.
(iv) Superior motor ability.

Terman and Ogden (1969) conducted studies and found that the gifted children are:

(i) Well adjusted in home and in school.
(ii) Emotionally fair, stable and self confident.
(iii) Have positive self-concept.
(iv) Leisure time activities are wide and varied.

James M. Dunlop stated positive and negative characteristics of gifted children. They are:

A. Positive Characteristics

1. Learn rapidly and easily.
2. Retain what they learn without much drill.
3. Show much curiosity in questioning.
4. Rich vocabulary marked by originality.
5. Enjoy reading.
6. Show interest in words and ideas.
7. Thinking based on reasoning.
8. Greater ability to generalize
9. Know and appreciate things of which normal children are unaware.
10. Interested in nature of man and universe at early stage.
11. Seek older companions

12. Possess a good sense of humour.
13. Have a desire to excel.

B. Negative Characteristics

1. Restless, disturbing and inattentive.
2. Careless and have poor handwriting.
3. Indifferent to class work.
4. Out spoken critical.

What the Problems do the Gifted Face?

In spite of Bloom's and Terman's findings, it would not be correct to say that every gifted child is superior in adjustment and emotional health.

Gifted Children have to Face the following Problems

1. Gifted adolescents especially girls are more likely to be depressed and to report social and emotional problems.
2. Many difficulties confront a gifted child including boredom frustration in school as well as in home. He/she feels isolated too from their peers as they ridicule him sometimes.
3. Gifted children may be impatient with friends, parents and even teachers who do not share their interests and abilities because their language is well developed. They may be seen as show off when they are simply expressing themselves.
4. They are sensitive to expectations and feelings of others so these students may be very vulnerable to criticisms and taunts.
5. Because they are goal directed and focused, so they may be stubborn and uncooperative.
6. Their keen sense of humour is used as a weapon against teachers and other students who create problems for them.
7. Adjustment problems seem to be greatest for the most gifted who are in the highest range of academic ability (above 180 I.Q.) (Hardman, 1999).

Teaching Strategies for Gifted Students

Identifying gifted children is not always easy and teaching them may be even more challenging. Many parents provide early educational experiences for their children even very advanced reading in the early grades but it does not guarantee that that they will still be outstanding readers later (Mills and Jackson,1990). Some educators believe that gifted students should be accelerated – moved quickly through the grades or through particular subjects. Other educators prefer enrichment—giving the students additional, more sophisticated and thought provoking work. But keeping them with their age mates in school, methods of teaching for gifted students should be adopted which may encourage abstract thinking, creativity, reading of high level books and original texts.

In working with gifted and talented students, a teacher must be imaginative, flexible, tolerant and unthreatened by the capabilities of these students. He must try to understand;

What do these children need most?
What are they ready to learn?
Who can help to challenge them?

Challenge and support are critical for all students. But challenging students who know more than any one else in the school about the subject can be a challenge. While challenging one should not forget support. There are three groups of students who are under represented in gifted students' education programmes:

1. Girls,
2. Students with learning disabilities, and
3. Students living in poverty (Stormont, Stebbins and Holliday, 2001).

1. Girls and Giftedness

As young girls develop their identities in adolescence, they often reject being labelled as gifted-being accepted and popular—fitting in many become more important than achievement (Stormont, *et al.*, 2001).

How can a Teacher Reach to Gifted Girls?

Here are some ideas given by the educationists.

1. Notice when girls' test scores seem to be declined in middle or high school.
2. Encourage assertiveness, achievement, high goals and demanding work from gifted girls.
3. Provide models of achievement through speakers, internships or readings.
4. Look for and support gifted girls in areas other than academic achievement.

2. *Gifted Students with Learning Disabilities (Twice-Exceptional)*

Here are some ideas for supporting twice-exceptional students (McCoach and Kehle, 2001).

1. Identify these students by looking longitudinally on their achievements.
2. Remedial skill deficits but also identify and develop talents and strengths.
3. Provide emotional support. It is important for all students but especially for this group.
4. Help students learn to compensate directly for their learning problems and assist them in 'tuning in' to their own strength and difficulties..

(3) *Gifted Students who Live in Poverty*

Health problems, lack of resources, homelessness, fears about safety and survival, frequent moves, responsibilities for the care of other family members it all makes them to achieve in school more difficult. Identify such gifted students:

1. Use alternative assessment, teacher's nomination and creativity tests.
2. Be sensitive to cultural differences in values about co-operative or solitary achievement (Ford, 2001).
3. Use multicultural strategies to encourage both achievement and the development of racial identities.

Educational Provisions

1. *Special Schools and Classes for Gifted Children*

Special classes and schools are universally accepted by the educationists for the education of gifted children. William Stern calls these classes as "Elite classes". However investigations revealed that it has yielded satisfactory results. But there is a very interesting controversy about the desirability of special education for the gifted. There are some valid points raised on either side of the issue. Some of the points advanced in favour of special classes are:

1. In special classes, gifted children are provided with the opportunity to work according to their superior ability but in average classes they are restrained as he moves at a slower pace and he does not get the benefit of superior teaching.
2. A group of gifted children have the advantage of progressing and developing more rapidly through mutual stimulation.

3. Special class offers opportunity to the gifted children for challenging work and develops their potentialities to the maximum.
4. Special classes provide opportunities to develop leadership in various fields. More developed and well-developed programmes become conducive for their talent and future leaders emerge in these particular fields.
5. Henry Goddard pointed out that gifted children are made of finer stuff than the majority. These children are more sensitive, alert and quick in their thinking. If they are not properly provided motivation and stimulation, they may create problems in the class. When they are put together with the average group, it becomes a problem for the teacher.

There is another group of psychologists and educationists who strongly refuted the isolation of gifted and talented children from regular schools and classes. They have their following reasons:

1. It is highly undemocratic "Equal opportunity of education should be provided to one and all".
2. Educationists point out that if gifted children are taken away from regular classes they tend to develop feeling of superiority and become snob and develop conceit.
3. Special classes give rise to a kind of intellectual aristocracy.
4. When gifted children are separated for the special class, an average child tends to lose but when working with the gifted he learns many things and becomes highly motivated.
5. It is felt that such programmes derive the society of superior leadership.

2. *Grade Skipping*

Grade skipping or double promotion was a technique to help the gifted to next higher class. This practice is no more in vogue now days. In view of the fact that it leaves a gap in acquisition of knowledge and allows a child younger in age to mix up with higher group. It is not desirable from social and personal adjustment point of view

3. *Acceleration and Enrichment Programme*

1. Acceleration strategies enable the gifted to select an educational programme which is challenging and interesting. No special curriculum has to be developed. It

does not have any negative effect on social, emotional or academic development.

2. In such a programme, gifted students are given additional materials to work with in the regular classroom settings. It may be consist of:
   (a) Provisions may be made for extra and co-curricular activities in the schools.
   (b) Introduction of interesting and new effective courses.
3. There have been number of approaches to teach gifted. Enrichment TRIAD is more popular approach among them developed by Renzulli (1977).

According to this model gifted children are given an effective educational environment that force them a choice for individual instruction. In this TRIAD:

(a) The teacher puts gifted children in contact with areas of study that are interesting and encourages them to explore the topic. It is known as General Exploratory Activity.

(b) The teacher provides training to the gifted children to develop thinking and reasoning skill to the area of study. It is called Group Training Activity.

(c) This is a Real Experimental Activity which is relevant for the gifted children. They investigate the real problem for the investigation.

4. *Non-Graded Classroom*

According to this system, the entire course of study is divided into series of units and arranged sequentially. Each child is free to complete the requirements of each stage and go on the principle of learning according to ability and its management and it is monitored through computer. However tutorial classes are meant to solve some specific learning problems. This system is quite popular in foreign countries but least in India.

Role of the Teacher in an Integrated Class

It is necessary that a teacher should be aware of the gifted child's feelings and his needs. They should be handled judiciously otherwise they may develop anxiety and feeling of insecurity. Some time gifted children do not accept their mistake as others have high expectations from them. In such circumstances, they should be helped and guided to set realistic goals to avoid unnecessary anxiety.

Cooperative planning provides an opportunity to the gifted children to develop their social potential as against rigid conformity of the typical class and repetitiveness. As such teacher should involve them in such planning activities.

Brain storming is also an effective method of encouraging the development of creative ideas. The role of the teacher is very important. He should not criticize ideas and accept all ideas in brain storming the problem is raised which generate as many ideas as possible to solve that problem.

The class teacher should also develop the problem solving and thinking skills by giving gifted children proper guidance. It should be an on-going activity of the classroom and be integrated to school experiences. A teacher must keep in mind that the regular curriculum can provide numerous opportunities for the development of creativity, problem solving and imaginatory thoughts so that inner potentials of gifted may come out.

Role of the Parents

Parents also play an important role in the proper development of the gifted children. It is important for the parents:

1. To provide the congenial and right environment for gifted children so that they may find scope to make good use of their intellectual ability.
2. They should not overlook their fundamental and psychological needs.
3. Such a child must feel that they are wanted by their parents and parents should enjoy their company.
4. Gifted child needs a lot of recognition especially of good deeds. They require sincere praise from their parents that makes them feel that they are liked.
5. Gifted child must feel that they are protected in case of need. Parents should encourage them in gaining new experiences.
6. Parents should keep themselves well informed about many facts, so that they can answer the child's questions readily and correctly.
7. Gifted child is always eager to know the answer of 'Why?", 'How'? 'When'? and 'Where'? etc., and answering of such questions will not only provide him the knowledge but satisfy his curiosity too as it is a strong urge.

QUESTIONS

A. Long Answer Type Questions

1. Define 'Exceptional children'. How many types of exceptional children are there? Discuss the steps that you take to educate gifted children.
2. Who is gifted child? Discuss various methods of identifying them.
3. Discuss various characteristics, needs and problems of the gifted children. Suggest a plan for their education.
4. 'Gifted are born not made'. Comment on it
5. Discuss causes giftedness. Enumerate the role of teachers and parents in educating them.

B. Short Answer Type Questions

1. Discuss programmes to educate gifted children.
2. Discuss the advantages and disadvantages of special classes.
3. Point out the adjustment problems of gifted children.
4. Discuss various causes of giftedness.
5. Define giftedness.

C. Objective Type Questions

1. The most ambitious systematic study on gifted children was conducted by

   (a) L.M. Terman *(b)* Laycock
   (c) Binet and Simon *(d)* D. Wechsler

2. Strong motivation rather than strong intellectual forces is the determinant of gifted, it has been stated by

   (a) L.M. Terman *(b)* Hollingsworth
   (c) Torrance *(d)* Freud

3. Educational psychologists are of the view that educational programme for gifted children are to include

   1. Acceleration 2. Grouping
   3. Enriching 4. Separation

   (a) 1, 2 and 4 are correct *(b)* All are correct
   (c) 12 and 3 are correct *(d)* 1, 2 and 4 are correct

4. Gifted children have positive self concept. True/False

5. Gifted children are:

   1. Academically superior 2. Emotionally stable.
   3. Well adjusted in home and school

   (a) 1 and 2 are correct *(b)* 2 and 3 are correct
   (c) 1 and 3 are correct *(d)* 12 and 3are correct

SUGGESTED READINGS

1. Backer, H.J. (1944). *Introduction to Exceptional Children,* New York, Macmillan.
2. Hewett, F.M. with Forness, S.R. (1984). *Education of Exceptional Learners* 3rd ed. Allyn & Bacon, Inc.
3. Hollingsworth, Leta. S. (1953). *Children Above 180 I.Q.* Yonkers and Hudson, World Book Co., New York.
4. Terman, L. M. *et al.* (1925). *Genetic Study of Genius,* Vol. 5, Stanford, California Standard University Press.
5. Witty, Paul, (1951). *The Gifted Child,* D.C. Heath and Co. Boston.

13

Creative Learners

No nation can afford to overlook or ignore the significance of creativity in this age of competition. Creative acts not only affect scientific and technological progress but also society in general. It is the responsibility of each nation to identify such talent and encourage and develop creative potential among the children. Now days researchers are eager to study cognitive processes, traits of personality, motivational patterns and background experiences to explain creativity of children. But to understand creativity, we must look to the social environment as it supports creativity. It was Guilford who first focused on creativity and concluded that creativity is a basic concern in the national interest. Torrance unravels unfailingly the positive domain in educational practice. Modern times, most psychologists and educationists are of the view that all persons have some creative potential, although there may be individual differences in degree.

Creativity is the process of developing original, novel and yet appropriate responses to a problem. An original response is one that is usually not given and it is one that is new or that has not precedence and should be appropriate if it is to be termed creative. Teresa Ambile (1996) proposes a three component model of creativity.

1. *Domain:* Relevant skills include talents and competencies that are valuable for working in the domain. An example would be one's skills in shaping something while one developed when lived with a family as a child (shaping stone, gold, silver etc.).
2. *Creativity:* Relevant process include work habits and

personality traits such as a habit of an individual working 10 hours a day to write and rewrite until he perfected his stories or poems.

3. *Intrinsic-task Motivation:* This type of creativity is greatly influenced by the social environment by supporting autonomy, stimulating curiosity, encouraging fantasy and providing challenge. Another social factor that influences on the creativity of children is whether the field is ready and willing to acknowledge the creative contribution.

The Nature of Creativity

Creativity is considered to be a greatest asset of mankind. It is important to understand the nature of creativity. It has been explained differently by different philosophers and psychologists. Philosophically a creative thinker is one whose thinking leads to a result which conforms to criteria of value in one domain or another. Artists deal only with appearances and not reality itself. The true artists bring into birth some new reality. They are creative as they enlarge human consciousness. Some of the psychologists equated creativity with mental health while some have related it to the personality development. Psychoanalysts like Freud restricted creativity to an interplay of unconscious and conscious mind.

Definitions of Creativity

Murray defined creativity in terms of product. According to him, "Creativity is the occurrence of something new and valuable. New he means a certain degree of novelty, originality related to sameness or replication and valuable he means either extrinsically or intrinsically valuable as such to one or more persons or generative of valuable composited in the future."

Guilford (1960) stressed on the divergent production, however he has conceptualized creativity in terms of mental abilities involved in creative pursuits.

He defined, "Creative thinking is a form of thought that is divergent." Divergent thinking occurs in response to problems that is yet not defined when no set way of solving the problem exists or is available. According to *Guilford*, the productions of new information from known information, or generation of logical possibilities, serves as the basis of creativity. The distinctive aspect of creative thinking is divergent thinking which is characterized by flexibility and fluency.

Lefton defined, "Creativity is a characteristic of thoughts and of problem solving, generally considered to include originality, novelty and appropriateness."

According to *Morris,* Creativity as a process involves three stages:

1. *Hypothesis Formation:* People try to formulate a new response to a problem. They have to explore the truth that have not been explored before and to think in new ways.
2. *Hypothesis Testing:* The hypothesis is tested using different tools and methods. If the result is novel, original and appropriate, the person can move toward the third stage *i.e.*
3. Communication of result.

Rogers defines, "Creativity is the emergence in action of a novel relational product growing out of the uniqueness of the individual." Uniqueness of the person, he means to man's tendency to actualize himself to express his potentialities.

According to *Stoddard,* "The creative act at its highest brings about notable differences in things, thoughts, work of art and social structures."

Torrance (1962) defined, "Creativity is the process of seeing problems or gaps in information, forming ideas or hypothesis testing and modifying these hypothesis and communication of the result."

In view of the above explanations and definitions, some of the psychologists have expressed creativity in terms of the product, while others in terms of process. However, it may be stated that there are at least five components of creativity which have been pointed out as:

1. The Act
2. The Process
3. The Object
4. The Person
5. The Environment.

1. The Act

The creative act can not be described but that is hypothesized as unknowable until it occurs. Rogers (1954) stressed on certain qualities that are associated with creative act. The creative person must undergo certain unique experiences, the first experience of the person is 'Eureka feeling.' This is so, I have discovered and this is what I wanted to express. Wertheimer suggested that creative thinking involved breaking down and restructuring over knowledge about a phenomenon in order to gain new insight into its nature.

Kelley and Rogers both maintained that we can be creative by gaining an insight into our own understanding of the subject. Actually creativity comes up when we arrange our thoughts in such a way that leads readily a different understanding of a situation.

2. *The Process*

The creative process is the emergence in action of a novel relational product resulting out of the uniqueness of the person. The creative process generally comes out with product which is novel. Every production is the result of a phased process but regarding to creativity it goes on in the unique manner. Graham Wallas identified four main stages to describe the creative process: *(i)* Preparation, *(ii)* Incubation, *(iii)* Illumination, and *(iv)* Verification.

- *(i)* *Preparation:* It is the period of accumulating necessary factual knowledge, skills or basic ideas but there is no guarantee-this stage will lead in generating creative ideas but each creative process has to pass from this stage.
- *(ii)* *Incubation:* This is the stage of relaxation turning attention away from the problem. However some kind of unconscious/ subconscious activity is going on although he seeks relaxation from conscious efforts.
- *(iii)* *Illumination:* It is marked with the sudden realization of the meaningful material comes to forefront and includes the psychological events and accompany the appearance of insight.
- *(iv)* *Verification:* The solution of the problem is tested and refined is known verification. This is the stage where the produced material gets the final or after testing the validity of the concepts.

3. *The Object*

The creativity is the object which generally referred to as the product. Here the quality is emphasized which should be originally related to the produced object. This originality is generally associated with four characteristics:

1. Novelty,
2. Unpredictability,
3. Uniqueness,
4. Surprise.

4. *The Person*

The person is explained in terms of conditions of self actualization with reference to the theory of personality of Maslow.

5. *The Environment*

It is the condition of openness which facilitates the creative person to move from the actual state of affairs towards the solution of the problem.

Characteristics of Creative Children

Torrance conducted a study to understand the characteristics of creative children. He found the followings:

1. *Courageous in Conviction:* He shows strong conviction in his belief and values. He is capable of going beyond socially conformist behaviour.
2. *Curiosity:* Creative child is very curious to know more and more about his environment.
3. *Independent Behaviour:* He is able to take independent judgment in crucial manner.
4. *Independent Thinking:* Creative child thinks independently to solve various types of problems.
5. *Busy in Doing Tasks:* He never leaves any task till he completes the same. All his energy is concentrated on the task in hand.
6. *Intuition:* He develops intuition in his problem.
7. Unwilling to accept routine solution.
8. High achievement motivation.
9. Willing to take risks.
10. *Visionary:* He has the vision of future problems.

Levels of Creativity

Taylor (1959) suggested following levels of creativity such as:

1. *Expressive Creativity:* It involves independent expression having originality in its essence. This is mostly exemplified in the spontaneous drawings of children.
2. *Productive Creativity:* This creativity calls for some production and mostly involved in artistic or scientific products.
3. *Inventive Creativity:* Ingenuity is displayed with material, methods and techniques. The inventors, explorers and discoverers are the example of using these types of creativity in their production.

4. *Innovative Creativity:* This is based upon highly developed abstract conceptualizing skills. Those who make significant modifications in basic foundations.
5. *Emergent Creativity:* This is the highest level of creativity. It is the ability which absorbs commonly provided experiences and produces something unique.

Personality Traits of Creative Learners

Psychologists have shown that it is the mixture/combination of intellectual factors and personality traits which distinguish the creative person from others. J.P. Guilford made the distinction between two types of thinking abilities one leading to intelligence *i.e.* convergent thinking and other leads creativity is called a divergent thinking.

Convergent thinking *Guilford* defines," convergent involves thinking towards our right answer. This type of thinking proceeds towards a restricted answer or solution.

Divergent Thinking

Guilford defines divergent thinking as a "kind of mental operation in which we think in different direction, sometimes seeking variety from known and remembered information. The very unique feature of this kind of thinking is that a variety of responses are produced.

Guilford also Mentioned Two Types of Traits

1. Aptitude Traits.
2. Non-Aptitude Traits.

1. Aptitude Traits

There are primary traits which are related to creativity. These traits have been come out by using factorial analysis:

A. Sensitivity to Problem

It is an ability that is reflected in a person's detection of something which is missing or lacking in a given situation or needs some modifications.

B. Fluency

This is a quantitative aspect of creativity, coming up with a large quantity of ideas, words and ways of expressing them. There are four factors associated with fluency of thinking such as:

(*a*) Word fluency,

(*b*) Associative fluency,

(*c*) Expressional fluency,

(*d*) Ideational fluency.

(*a*) *Word Fluency:* It is an ability to express words having a specific letter or combination of words.

(*b*) *Associative Fluency:* It involves a requirement of meaning for the words given. This ability requires for generating associations or relation, production of analogies or similarities.

(*c*) *Expressional Fluency:* This is an ability which involves the production of phrases or sentences.

(*d*) *Ideational Fluency:* This ability involves production of ideas.

C. Flexibility of Thinking

Flexibility means to think up a variety of ideas and new ways of dealing with situations. It expresses how an individual responds in different ways to a stimulus.

D. Originality

It is manifested as uncommon with respect to figural, verbal or symbolic transformations. We may say that there are two types of responses-one is obvious and other is remote. Obvious response shows ideational fluency while remote response indicates originality.

E. Redefinition

It is ability of rearranging ideas, concepts, objects or to state the use of parts in new ways. Improvision reflects this ability.

F. Elaboration

This ability is an expression of detailed steps of production, variety of implications and consequences that can be measured quantitatively.

2. *Non-Aptitude Traits*

The traits of motivation and temperament are said to have determining effects upon creative performance. Anne Roe (1946, 1953) concluded in her studies that willing to work hard and to work long hours stood out in common among individuals who showed creativity in arts and science.

Theories of Creative Performance

Different psychologists and philosophers tried to answer certain questions related to creativity. The answers constitute various theories of creativity. These are based upon simple assumptions while have made under gone empirical validations. Some important theories on creative performance have been mentioned here:

1. *Divine Inspiration Theory:* Some philosophers have considered creativity as divine inspiration. Plato considers the writer as an agent of some higher power. It is only the higher power which makes him/her capable of producing any thing creative. Most of the creative persons like poets have often experienced that there is some invisible power that makes them to create something new (Houseman, 1933).
2. *Accidental Theory:* Much of the creativity is the result of accident or chance although this theory fails to provide any scientific basis of explanation however one thing is sure that no creativity is possible unless one is intensely interested and motivated in it. Undoubtedly chance plays important role but it is only achievement motivation that makes every creation possible.

Besides above, there are psychologists who attempted to explain creative performance in their theory of personality. These are grouped in following four categories:

1. Psychoanalytic theory of personality.
2. Humanistic theory of personality.
3. Cognitive theory.
4. Behaviouristic theory.

1. Psycho-analytic Theory of Personality

(a) *Sigmund Freud:* The father of psychoanalysis was the first who attempted to analyze the process of creativity. He and his followers lay special stress on his repressed wishes, pre-genital and libidinal urges, the sublimation of which largely determines creativity. The creativity owes its origin to conflict within the unconscious mind. According to him, creativity helps a conflict ridden person in releasing his inner conflicts. Freudians are also of the view that creativity is a recapitulation of early childhood experiences.

(b) *Compensatory Theory:* Adler is the exponent of this theory, according to him, human beings produce art, science and other aspects of creative performance to compensate for their own inadequacies.

(c) Jung is another very important theorist whose contribution to creativity is quite substantial. He viewed creativity at two levels: *(i)* The psychological mode, and *(ii)* The visionary mode.

(i) *The Psychological Mode:* In the psychological mode the content is mainly derived from the domain of human consciousness in relation to family, environment, society and social institutions but the release of creativity does not transcend the limits of psychological intelligibility.

(ii) *The Visionary Mode:* In this mode the content is derived from the timeless depths which Jung called the collective unconscious.

2. *Humanistic Theory of Personality or Motivational Theory*

A group of motivation theorists believe that man's basic motivational tendency is towards self-actualization or self-fulfillment. According to Maslow, creativity is a maximum of self -actualizing which stresses personality and its achievements. Self-actualizing people are highly motivated and unfrightened by the unknown, mysterious and the puzzlings. For Rogers, motivation is the mainspring of creativity. It is a tendency within a man to actualize him, to express/expose his potentialities and to activate all the capacities of the organism. According to him this tendency exists in every individual and awaits only the proper condition to be exposed. Motivation may be intrinsic or extrinsic but both are necessary conditions to creativity.

3. *Behaviouristic Theory or Theory of Association*

Associanists base their theory of creativity on stimulus-response associations. According to them, creativity results from unusual associations. Mednick is the exponent of this theory. According to him, "creative process is the forming of associate element units into new combinations which either meet specified requirements or in some useful." On the basis of this conceptualization, he developed a test of Creative Remote Association Test.

4. *Cognitive Theory*

Cognitive psychologists assume that an individual's behaviour is always based on cognition – the act of knowing about the situation where the behaviour occurs. Gestalts like Wertheimer use the terms productive thinking and problem solving to creativity. According to him, productive thinking involves a process of successive restructuring of a problem.

Guilford also discusses the concept of creativity as a cognitive ability, multivariate in nature. He revealed quite a number of components that constitute creative thinking. Guilford analyses the nature of creative thinking ability which he equates with divergent thinking.

The Structure of Intellect Model propounded by Guilford seems to be more rational and widely accepted as it provides the ground to measure creativity quantitatively with the help of divergent thinking test. Secondly, it considers the motivational factor as an important determinant of creativity. Thirdly, the model assumes that every individual is in possession of creative thinking ability.

Relationship Between Creativity and Intelligence

Conceptual Identification: Guilford (1950) conceptualized creativity as divergent thinking process whereas intelligence has been associated with convergent thinking and the difference provides two independent cognitive as two independent components (between which relationship can be established. Torrance (1963) as well as Getzels and Jackson (1962) believed that the conventional tests of intelligence fail to measure divergent production abilities. The relative difference between intelligence and creativity *i.e.* between convergent and divergent thinking as conceptualized by Guilford (1950, 1956 and 1959) in his S I Model. It can be best explained in terms of their symbolic presentation. Guilford's concept of Model stresses on the divergent thinking and information rather than the convergent production and evaluation so for as creativity is concerned.

Measurement Creativity

The creativity tests are usually open ended. The examiners ask how many solutions the subject can see instead of one solution.

Creative Tests

1. Torrance Test of Creative Thinking.
2. Christensen-Guilford Test.
3. Mednick's Remote Association Test.
4. Passi's Battery of Creativity Test.
5. Baquer Mehandi's Test of Creativity.

Educational Provision for Creative Children

Creativity in the Classroom

Classroom teaching is the most powerful instrument which can help students to develop the creative talent maximum. Teachers are to take responsibility by shifting from a mere routine type of teaching to creative teaching. Creative teaching is possible when teachers become more creative in helping their learners to be creative. It means teachers should give more attention to creative problem skills of the students. The role of the teacher is to stimulate, guide to provide a conducive environment and the necessary equipment where students have not to be only passive listeners instead they should be active particulars in teaching-learning-process.

Most of the researchers are of the view that creativity should not be left to chance for its development instead it should be fostered through deliberate methods. Teachers should find out methods, approaches and techniques that may be employed to assist students to think creatively. In this regard teachers must know the factors that inhibit creative thinking among students. Winner (2000) lists four dangers to avoid:

1. Avoid pushing so hard that the child's intrinsic passion to master a field becomes a craving for extrinsic rewards.
2. Avoid pushing so hard that the child later looks back on a missed childhood.
3. Avoid freezing the child into safe, technically perfect way of performing that has led to lavish rewards.
4. Be aware of the psychological wounds that can follow when the child who can perform perfectly becomes the forgotten adult who can do nothing more than continue to perform perfectly without—ever creating something new.

Teachers and parents can encourage students with outstanding abilities and creative talents to give back to the society that has provided extra support and resources. Besides above dangers teachers should eliminate such obstacles which interfere in developing creativity such as:

1. The pressure to conform is the main obstacle in eliciting creative responses.
2. Authoritarian attitudes suppress the creative potential.
3. Threats and ridicules injure the feelings of self-worth in students and that block in the outlet of their creative potential.
4. External evaluation arouses defensive attitudes among students that inhibit creative responses.

5. Inflexible defene mechanisms and compulsive fears from the part of teachers deter the productive thinking among students.
6. Teacher's demand for right answers creates an obstacle in creativity.

Creative Teacher

A creative teacher is one who invents such creative techniques which are unforeseeable and put the students in surprise. Such techniques create interest, sustain the attention and induce to think off in different direction to the students in order to get the large number of solutions to the problem. A creative teacher may apply the following techniques in the classroom to develop creativity among students.

1. *Self-initiated Learning:* Teachers may provide freedom of thought to elicit creative responses.
2. *Provision of Permissive Learning Environment:* Democratic teaching-learning environment facilitates creative learning that also leads to creativity.
3. *Motivation to Creative Thought Process:* The creative teacher motivates students to imagine, to think for various solutions to problems and allow seeking for new associations among existing objects.
4. *Intellectual Fluency and Flexibility:* The creative teacher stimulates students to store the information and use it in different situations.
5. *Accept and Encourage Divergent Thinking:* Creative teacher lays stress on divergent thinking instead of convergent thinking *e.g.* during classroom discussions he may ask—Can any one suggest a different way of looking at this question?
6. *Tolerate Dissent*: Creative teacher should develop a habit of tolerating dissent expression from the students.
7. Encourage students to trust their own judgement.
8. Emphasis that everyone is capable to create in some form.
9. *Develop Curiosity:* The creative teachers foster curiosity and encourage their students to make the best use of the question. Operational questions always lead to exploration which foster curiosity.
10. Active participation is essential for the students as well as teachers.

11. Be a stimulus to the students for creative thinking.
12. *To be Adventurous:* The creative teacher inculcates the spirit of adventure among his students. He allows them to face uncertainties and ambiguities of life as a challenge which are important traits of personality to be a creative.

Techniques of Development of Creativity

It has been realized that creative thinking abilities can be developed to varying degrees among different individuals through systematically organized programmes in the schools. There are various techniques such as:

1. Attribute listing.
2. Morphological analysis.
3. Brain storming.
4. Inquiry training.
5. Synectics.

1. Attribute Listing

This technique was developed in 1954 by Robert Platt Crawford. According to him magic inspiration is not the only, even major source of creativity. Most of the creativity arises from changing the attributes of an object or an activity or from grafting on to the object or an activity of an attribute or attributes of some other object of activity.

In attributing listing, the attempt is made first to list the basic but modifiable attributes or properties or specifications of a particular object or activity, after that an attempt is made to search for alternatives to present attribute. This is a kind of search for a better method of solving human problems. This technique is very much applied for improving product design to attract consumers. Crawford laid down the following principle of attribute listing:

(i) Creation is largely adaptation and experimentation.
(ii) Creation is useful modification of an attribute or assimilation of attributes of other objects.
(iii) Creation is the continuing array of modification suggested by ideas.
(iv) It is described to search for concrete alternatives during the process of modifying the current attributes of an object.
(v) Creativity can be systematized by looking first for closely related substitutes of the current attribute and then progressively going in for more and more far out alternatives.

2. *Morphological Analysis*

This is a variant of attribute listing. This technique was developed by Fred Zincky in California in 1957. It provides facilitation of imagination by allowing the individual to focus on one aspect of the object or activity at one time. It combines the modifiable attributes of the major variables of problems into a grid so that all the possible combinations can be considered. In morphological analysis the basic is to identify the critical modifiable attributes and listing several attributes for each of the attributes enable one to generate a very large number of alternatives of an object or an activity. The difference between "attribute listing" and "morphological analysis" is that former works best when the object, activity or product is sought to be modified while later can also be applied profitable to modify general objects or activities. Both are not merely techniques, they embody important values and attitude favouring creativity.

3. *Brain Storming*

Alex Osborm (1957) developed this method of brain storming which is being widely used and it has now become the tremendous source of generating creative power. It is a technique in which problem is attacked from all possible angles to generate a large number of ideas in order to arrive at the best solution.

In a brain storming session a group of students sit around a table to brain storm a specific problem. Each participant presents the ideas which come in his mind. No member of the group is allowed to criticize on the idea put forward by another member. The main objective which underline is that offering a person from the usual inhibitions that operate to block his creative process. Encouraging creativity through everyday interaction with students, teachers should use this technique of brain storming. As mentioned earlier, the basic tenet of brain storming is to separate the process of creating ideas from the process of evaluating them because evaluation inhibits creativity. Evaluation, discussion and criticism are postponed until all possible suggestions have been made. In such situation, one idea inspires others; students do not withhold potentially creative solutions out of fear of criticism. John Bech (1997) give following the rules for brain storming:

1. Defer judgment.
2. Avoid ownership of ideas.
3. Feel free to hitch hike on other ideas. This means that one

may borrow elements from ideas already on the table to make slight modifications of ideas already suggested.

4. Encourage wild ideas.

This technique is useful and practical. Teachers and students can use it very successfully to find out the best solutions to the problems that are being challenged by the existing system of education.

4. Inquiry Training

This model was developed by Richard Suchman (1962) to teach students. It is a process investigating and explaining unusual phenomenon. He identified the components of the inquiry process and built them into the instrumental model to which he called 'Inquiry Training'. His approach is based on four postulates:

(i) *Children are Curious by Nature:* Any puzzling problem is motivated them to explore the answer of the problem.

(ii) This process of inquiry can be taught to students as they can learn scientific procedures directly to solve the problem scientifically.

(iii) *Team approach:* This approach is more useful than the individual approach to find the solution to a problem.

(iv) *All Knowledge is Tentative:* The students should be made aware of this fact as there is always scope of modification.

5. Synectics

The word synectics has been derived from the Greek Word 'Synecticos' which means joining together two different and apparently diverse elements. Gordon (1960) is the originator of this method. It is an operational theory for the conscious use of the preconscious and psychological mechanisms present in man's creative activity. Synectics is defined as the mental activity in problem solving in order to arrive at solution of fundamental novelty. Gordon basically put forward three assumptions about this creative process viz.

(i) Creative process could be described and it be enhanced by conscious efforts to promote the creative process among students.

(ii) Emotional component was more important than the intellectual. Similarly the irrational is more important than the rational.

(iii) Emotional and irrational elements must be understood in order to increase the probability of success in a problem solving situation.

Gordon found that there are five interrelated states of mind should be present in an individual to move through the creative process so that he may make a break through to contribute to a final solution. They are:

1. Detachment and involvement
2. Deferment
3. Speculations
4. Autonomy
5. Hedonic response.

The objective of synectics training should be provided to teachers in view of the factors mentioned above. The following activities, approaches and techniques should be used to develop creativity among students.

1. *Metaphoric Activities:* Metaphors establish a relationship of likeness, the comparison on one object or idea with another object or idea by using one another. It introduces a conceptional distance between the student and the object or subject matter and allows time to think reflectively. During this activity students innovate and imagine.
2. *Evocative Questions:* Teachers may ask such questions which are open ended queries intending to draw all the students of the class into creative process such designed questions may start discussion and arouse interest among students.
3. *Direct Analogous Questions:* Direct analogous questions are a simple comparison of two objects or concepts. Such questions may not be identical in all respects.
4. *Personal Analogy:* It involves the students emphatically with the ideas or object to be compared.

QUESTIONS

A. Long Answer Type Questions

1. Explain the concept of creativity. Discuss various factors related to it.
2. Discuss various theories of creativity. Do you agree that every child is creative?
3. Discuss in detail the significance of creativity in education.
4. What is creativity? How can it be identified?

5. Discuss in detail the role of the teacher in the development of creativity among children.

B. Short Answer Type Questions

1. State the relationship between creativity and intelligence.
2. Discuss the role of imagination in creativity.
3. Differentiate between creativity and creative thinking.
4. Differentiate between convergent and divergent thinking.
5. What is brain storming?
6. Write a note on synectics.

C. Objective Type Questions

1. A technique for problem solving that involves considering all possible solution with making prior evaluative judgments is known:
   (*a*) Mediation (*b*) Hypothesis testing
   (*c*) Brain storming (*d*) Creativity.
2. Creativity is a process involving three stages hypothesis formulation, hypothesis testing and communication of research. It has been defined by:
   (*a*) Guilford (*b*) Morris Stein
   (*c*) Johnson (*d*) Mackinnon
3. Thinking occurs in response to a problem that as yet is not defined when any set way of solving the problem exists or available is called
   (*a*) Convergent thinking (*b*) Conceptual thinking
   (*c*) Divergent thinking (*d*) Hypothetical thinking.
4. Consider the statements:
   1. Creativity is an expression of the psychologically healthy person.
   2. Creative persons are not deliberate non-conformists.
   3. Creative persons are genuinely independent.
   4. Creative persons are more introverted.

   (*a*) 1, 2, and 4 are correct (*b*) 2, 3, and 4 are correct
   (*c*) All are correct (*d*) 1, 3 and 4 are correct.
5. There is a four stage theory of creative thinking which held those periods of:
   1. Incubation 2. Preparation
   3. Illumination 4. Verification.

   Correct sequence is

   (*a*) 1, 3, 2, 4 (*b*) 1, 2, 3, 4
   (*c*) 2, 1, 3, 4. (*d*) 2, 3, 1, 4.
6. Four state theory of creative thinking was formulated by

(*a*) Graham Wallas (*b*) Helmholtz
(*c*) Barron *et al* (*d*) Mackinnon

7. An investigation of 151 fifth grade children was made to establish relationship between intelligence and creativity. It was conducted by
   (*a*) J. P. Guilford (*b*) Wallach and Kogan
   (*c*) Barron et al (*d*) Graham Wallas
8. Sensitivity to problems, originality, and ingenuity are the components of creativity. It is stated by
   (*a*) Wallas (*b*) Johnson
   (*c*) Davis (*d*) Barron
9. Divergent thinking is opposite to conceptual thinking. True/False
10. There are factors that have negative effect on creativity.
    1. Emotional factors 2. Set
    3. Functional fixedness

    (*a*) 1 and are correct (*b*) 2 and 3 are correct
    (*c*) 1 and 3 are correct (*d*) all are correct.

SUGGESTED READINGS

1. Cattel, R.B. and Butcher, H.J. (1970). Creativity and Personality, Vernon, P.E. *Modern Psychological Readings* Penguin.
2. Getzels, J.W. and P.W. Jackson (1962). *Creativity and Intelligence Exploration with Gifted Students.* New York, John Wiley and Sons, Inc.
3. Guilford, J.P. (1959). "Traits and Creativity". In P.E. Vernon (ed), *Creativity Penguin Modern Psychological Reading,* England, 1970.
4. Hammer, E.F. (1961). *Creativity,* New Yoık, Random House.
5. Johnson, D.M. (1948). *Essential of Psychology,* New York, McGraw Hill Book Co.
6. Parmesh, C.R. (1972). *Creativity and Personality,* Madras, Janta Book House.
7. Thorndike, R.L. (1996). *Measurement of Creativity,* New York Teachers College record.
8. Torrance, E.P. (1962). *Guiding Creative Talent,* Eagle Wood Cliffs, New Jersey, Prentice Hall, Inc.
9. Wallach, M.A. (1971). *The Intelligence – Creativity Distinction,* New York, General Learning Press.

14

Disorders of Childhood and Adolescence

Disruptive Behaviour

(i) Attention-Deficit/Hyperactivity Disorder (see Chapter 7)
(ii) Oppositional Defiant Disorder and Conduct Disorder.
(iii) Anti-social Personality Disorder.

The group of disorders centers on a child's or an adolescent's relationship to social norms and rules of conduct. In both conduct disorders and oppositional defiant disorder, aggressive or anti-social behaviour is the focus. As we will see, oppositional defiant disorders are usually apparent by about age 6 while conduct disorders tend to be seen by age 9. Both disorders are closely limited children showed the aggressive behaviour and rule violation that often are labelled conduct disorders and many came into contact with the authorities as a result of this delinquent behaviour. There is substantial evidence that in some children disruptive behaviour problems develop gradually from childhood onward in an orderly fashion (Loeber, *et al.*, 1992). Fortunately however not all children who are described as having conduct disorders or who engage in delinquent behaviour grow up to become anti-social personalities or commit themselves to lives of crime.

Oppositional Defiant Disorders

An important precursor of the anti-social behaviour seen in children who develop conduct disorder is often what is now called oppositional defiant disorder (Biederman, Faraone *et al.*, 1996). The essential feature is a recurrent pattern of negativistic, defiant, disobedient and hostile behaviour toward authority. This order begins usually by the age of six, whereas full-blown conduct disorder does not typically begin until the age of nine or later. Prospective studies have found a developmental sequence from oppositional defiant disorder to conduct disorder, with common risk factors for both conditions (Hinshaw, 1994). That is virtually all cases of conduct disorder were preceded developmentally by oppositional defiant disorder. The risk factors for both include family discord, socio-economic disadvantage and anti-social behaviour in the parents (Hinshaw, 1994).

A pattern over at least a six month period, of negativistic, hostile, and defiant behaviour that includes at least four of the following:

1. Having frequent loss of temper.
2. Having frequent arguments with adults.
3. Deliberately defiant or non-compliant with rules and results.
4. Deliberately annoying others.
5. Blaming others for own behaviour.
6. Touchy and easily annoyed.
7. Angry and resentful.
8. Spiteful or vindictive.

These behaviours must be serious enough to interfere with functioning in some area – social, school, or work.

ODD behaviours are usually seen first at home and then may generalize to other settings. Family factors may play a role in ODD. Other factors that may be important are the way parents help their children to become socialized or to modulate their behaviour according to the demands of the situation (Frick, 1993).

Conduct Disorder

The essential symptomatic behaviour in the conduct disorder involves persistent repetitive violation of rules and a disregard for the rights of others. Conduct disordered children slow or deficit in social behaviour. In general, they manifest such characteristics as overt or covert hostility quarrelsomeness, vengefulness and destructiveness. Lying, solitary stealing and temper tantrum are common. Such children tend to be sexually uninhibited and inclined toward sexual aggressiveness. Zoccolille, Meyers and Assiter (1997) found that conduct disorder was a risk factor for unwed pregnancy and substance abuse in teenage girls.

Behaviour Features of Conduct Disorder

Three or more of these behavioural criteria must have been present in the last 12 months and at least one in the past 6 months.

Aggression toward people including bullying, intimidating, use of weapons, physical cruelty, forced sexual activity mugging, purse-snatching, and aggression toward animals.

1. Destruction of property, including fire-setting and other deliberate property destruction.
2. Deceitfulness or theft, including breaking into a building or car, conning others to obtain goods, stealing items of value.
3. Serious rule violation: including staying out at night without parents' permission before age 13, running away from home school truancy before age 13.
4. These behaviours must be severe enough to cause impairment in some area of functioning—social, school, or work.

Causal Factors in Conduct Disorder

1. *A Self-Perpetuating Cycle:* Evidence has accumulated that a genetic predisposition leading to low verbal intelligence, mild neuropsychological problems and difficulties temperament can set the stage for early-onset conduct disorder through a self perpetuating mechanisms (Slutsky, Heath *et al.*, 1997). The child's difficult temperament may lead to an insecure attachment because parents find it hard to engage in the good parenting that would lead to a secure attachment. In addition low verbal intelligence and other deficits, which may involve deficiencies in self-control functions such as sustaining attention, planning self-monitoring, inhibiting unsuccessful or impulsive behaviour-may help to set the stage for a life-long course of difficulties.
2. *Age of Onset and Anti-social Personality Disorder:* Children who develop conduct disorder at an earlier age are much more likely to develop psychopathic or anti-social personality disorder as adult than are adolescents who develop conduct disorder suddenly in adolescence (Hinshaw, 1994; Moffitt, 1993b). Thus, it is the pervasiveness of the problems first associated with oppositional defiant disorder and then with conduct disorder, which is the pattern, associated an adult diagnosis of psychopathic or antisocial personality disorder.

Most adolescents who develop conduct disorder in adolescence, do not go on to become adult psychopathic or anti-social personality but instead have problems limited to the adolescent years

3. *Environmental Factors:* The genetic or constitutional liabilities that may predispose to conduct disorder and adult psychopathic and anti-social personality, Kazdin (1995) underscored the importance of family and social context factors as causal variables in conduct disorder. Environment factors may interact as the child who was rejected by his peers because they did not like his overly aggressive behaviour. The children who are aggressive socially unskilled are often rejected by their peers and such rejection can lead to 'a spiraling sequence' of social interactions with peers that exacerbates the tendency toward anti-social behaviour (Dodgem, 1980; Coie and Lenox, 1994). These socially rejected sub-groups of aggressive children are also at the highest risk for adolescent delinquency and probably for adult antisocial personality. The combination of rejection by parents, peers and teachers leads these children to become isolated and alienated. Not surprisingly they often turn to deviant peer groups for companionship (Coie and Lenox, 1994).

Investigators generally seem to agree that the family setting of a conduct-disordered child is typically characterized by ineffective parenting, rejection, harsh, and inconsistent discipline and often parental neglect (Frick, 1998). Frequently. the parents have an unstable marital relationship (Osborn,1992), are emotionally disturbed or sociopathic, and do not provide the child with consistent guidance, acceptance or affection. Recently Patterson (1996) concluded that parents who are themselves apprised as having anti-social characteristics are very likely to be ineffective in their parental skills.

Family discord, such as conflict and disharmony accompanying divorce can be instrumental in the development of conduct disorder (Chess and Thomas, 1984; Robins, 1991). Regardless of whether the family is intact, a child in a conflict-charged home feels overtly rejected. Rutter and Quinton (1984b) concluded that family discord and hostility were the primary factor defining the relationship between disturbed parents and disturbed children; this is particularly true with respect to the development of conduct disorders in children and adolescents. Such discord and hostility are conceptualized as contributing to poor and ineffective parenting skills—especially ineffective discipline and supervision. These children are trained by the family directly in anti-social behaviour by coercive interchanges and indirectly by lack of monitoring and consistent discipline (Capaldi and Patterson, 1994, p. 169).

Besides these above mentioned familial factors, a number of broader psychosocial and socio-cultural variables increase the probability that a child will develop conduct disorder and later adult psychopathic or anti-social personality disorder. Low SES, poor neighbouring, parental stress and depression all appear to increase the likelihood that a child will become enmeshed in this cycle (Capaldi and Patterson, 1994).

Treatment and Outcomes

The treatment for oppositional defiant disorder and conduct disorder tends to focus on the dysfunctional family patterns described above and on finding ways to alter the child's aggressive or otherwise maladaptive behaviours.

The Cohesive Family Model

Therapy for a conduct disordered child is likely to be ineffective unless some means can be found for modifying the child's environment. The effective treatment strategy with conduct disorder in children is the cohesive family model (Patterson *et al.*, 1991).

In this family group oriented approach parents' of conduct disordered children are viewed as lacking in parenting skills and has having failed to socialize the children by behaving in inconsistent ways, thereby reinforcing inappropriate behaviour. Children learnt escape or avoid parental criticism by escalating their negative behaviour. It is the responsibility of the parents to pay their positive attention to modify the reasons which are lying in developing conduct disorder. Reinforcement which helps a child to change his or her attitude is praiseworthy. All the negative character/conduct should be demotivated and deconditioned.

Behavioural Techniques

The advent of behaviour therapy techniques has made the outlook brighter or children who manifest conduct disorders. Teaching control techniques to the parents of such children is important, so that they function as therapists in reinforcing desirable behaviour and modifying the environmental conditions that have been reinforcing maladaptive behaviour. The change brought about when they consistently accept and reward their child's behaviour and stop focusing attention on the negative behaviour may finally change their perception and feelings toward the child leading to the basic acceptance that the child has so badly needed.

QUESTIONS

A. Long Answer Type Questions

1. Explain the concept of "Oppositional Defiant Disorder." Discuss its symptoms.
2. What are the causes of oppositional defiant disorder? How can a teacher help in eradicating this disorder?
3. Explain the term "Conduct Disorder". Discuss its various causes.
4. What are the behavioural features of Conduct Disorder? Discuss.
5. What treatments should be adopted by the therapist? Discuss.

B. Short Answer Type Questions

1. The Cohesive family model is one of the effective therapies. Discuss
2. Effect of environment on conduct disorder.
3. Discuss causes of conduct disorder.
4. Describe a self perpetuating cycle.
5. Treatment and outcomes of conduct disorder.

C. Objective Type Questions

1. The group of disorders centers on a child's or an adolescent's relationship to____________norms and____________conduct.
2. Aggression is the focus point of conduct disorder. True / False
3. Conduct disordered child's behaviour includes
   (i) blame others for own behavioural misconduct.
   (ii) He is touchy and easily annoyed.
   (a) (i) is true, (ii) is false *(b)* (i) is correct, (ii) is wrong
   (c) both are correct *(d)* both are wrong
4. The essential symptomatic behaviour in the conduct disorder involves persistent repetitive violation of____________.

SUGGESTED READINGS

1. Munsinger, Harry (1983). *Principles of Abnormal Psychology*, Macmillan Publishing, New York.
2. Coleman, C. (1976). *Abnormal Psychology and Modern Life* (5th Ed.), D. B. Taraporevala Sons & Co. Pvt. Ltd.
3. Mussen, P.H. & Others (1970). *Child Development and Personality* (3rd Ed.) A Harper International edition Tokyo.

4. Shanker, Uday (1970). *Personality Development,* Atma Ram & Sons Delhi.
5. Liebert, R. M. & Others (1979). *Developmental Psychology,* Prentice-Hall of India Pvt. Ltd., New Delhi.
6. Barlow. H. & Durand, V. Mark. (1998). *Abnormal Psychology* (2nd Ed.) Brooks/Cole Publishing Company U.S.A.
7. Holland, Morris K. (1981). *Introductory Psychology,* D.C. Heath and Company, Toronto.
8. Sarason & Sarason, B. R. *Abnormal Psychology – The Problem of Maladaptive Behaviour,* Prentice-Hall of India Pvt. Ltd., New Delhi.

15

Anti-Social Personality Disorder

The terms anti-social and psychopathic personality sometimes used interchangeably to refer to personality characteristics and behaviour patterns that lead to serious difficulties in interpersonal relationships and usually bring the individual into repeated conflict with society. Their outstanding characteristics are a marked lack of ethical or moral development and an inability to follow approved models of behaviour. Basically they are unsocialized and incapable of significant loyalty to other persons, groups or social values. Hostile psychopaths who are prone to act out their impulses in remorseless and often senseless violence. In other cases, anti-social or psychopathic persons show periods of reliability and are capable of assuming responsibility and pursuing long-range goals, but they do so in unethical way with a complete lack of consideration for the rights and well-being of others.

The individuals possessing average or superior intellectual ability who are neither neurotic nor psychotic but are socially misfit and borderline mental cases are labelled psychopathic or anti-social personalities or constitutional psychopathic inferiors. It includes:

1. Pathological liars,
2. Sexual perverts,
3. Tramps,
4. Amoral individuals,
5. Misanthropes,
6. Eccentrics, and
7. Certain types of emotionally unstable individuals.

Little is known concerning the cause of this disorder. It is generally assumed that constitutional factors consisting of heredity defects and disturbed parent-child relationships in early childhood play important role.

Dunn, W.H. and Henderson, D.K. listed the most outstanding characteristics of this disorder:

1. Intelligence is not affected and the symptoms do not correspond to those noted in psychoses or psychoneurosis.
2. The unchecked pursuit of pleasure expressed by the immediate gratification of needs and desires irrespective of consequences to self or others is the dominant life motive.
3. Their actions appear to others to indicate lack of foresight, poor judgment and inability to profit from experience.
4. Psychopaths exhibit disorders of conduct of an anti-social or a social nature, thoughtless of the welfare of others; and seize every opportunity to deceive and exploit associates.
5. Their lives lack stability, direction and tenacity of purpose.
6. Psychopaths are generally described as cold, callous, shallow, cruel, infantile and flighty.
7. Sexual development is usually retarded or abnormal. Perversions of all types are common and these are accepted without shame or conflict.
8. Almost all are selfish, stubborn and egocentric.

The person whose behaviour seems to be odd or abnormal which a source of distress for him and others is known as anti-social personality disorder.

Such symptoms were described by J.C. Prichard in 1837. He called it "moral insanity" because the intellect of such persons was normal but the moral values were depraved, after this work, clinicians used the term" 'constitutional psychopathic personality' to label such behaviour. By 1920's such a person was labelled as having psychopath and sociopath personality. The American Psychiatric Association coined the term anti-social personality in the late 1960's. H. Cleckley's in his book, *The Mask of Sanity* written in 1964 describes about anti-social person. He includes criteria to recognize such personalities:

As lack of remorse or shame, unreliability, untruthfulness and insincerity.

Some other Characteristics of Anti-Social Behaviour

1. Psycho-analytic Interpretation

Psychoanalysts stressed the importance of unconscious motives and repressed mental conflicts. A repressed sexual wish may be indirectly gratified by some substitute forbidden and exciting act such as stealing. A secret hatred of the father may be expressed by a general defiance of authority.

2. Inadequate Conscience Development

Psychopaths appear unable to understand and accept ethical values except on a verbal level. However they claim to adhere to high moral standards that have no apparent connection with their behaviour. In short, their conscience development is severely retarded or nonexistent although their intellectual development is typically normal.

3. Irresponsible and Impulsive Behaviour

Psychopaths generally have a callous disregard for the rights, needs and well-being of others. They often break law impulsively and without regard for the consequences. They seldom forgo immediate pleasure for future gains and long-range goals. They live in the present without realistically considering either past or future.

4. Rejection of Authority

Psychopaths behave as if social regulations do not apply to them. They do not play by the rules of the game. Frequently, they have a history of difficulties with educational andlaw enforcement authorities.

5. Ability to Impress and Exploit Others

Psychopaths are often charming and likeable with a disarming manner that easily wins friends. They have typically a good sense of humour and an optimistic outlook. The frequent liars usually seem sincerely sorry if caught in a lie, and promise to make amends but - will not do so. They have good insight into other people's needs and weaknesses and are adept at exploiting them.

6. Inability to Maintain Good Relationships

Psychopaths are seldom able to keep close friends. Irresponsible and egocentric, they are usually cynical, unsympathetic, ungrateful and remorseless in their dealings. Violence toward family members is common. Manipulative and exploitative in sexual relationships, psychopaths are irresponsible and unfaithful mates. Although they often promise to change, they rarely do so for long.

Causal Factors in Psychopaths/Anti-Social Personality

1. Genetic Influences

There are studies that show a modest heritability for anti-social or criminal behaviour (Carey & Goldman, 1997). Researches also note that strong environmental influences interact with genetic predispositions to determine which individuals become criminals or anti-social personalities (Lykken, 1995; Goldman and Carry 1997).

2. *Deficient Aversive Emotional Arousal and Conditioning*

Research evidence indicates that psychopaths show deficient aversive emotional arousal, this condition presumably renders them less prone to fear and anxiety in stressful situations and less prone to normal conscience development and socialization. This lack of anxiety is more associated with the egocentric callous, exploitative dimension of psychopaths rather than with the anti-social behaviour dimension which may have a slight positive association with anxiety (Frick, 1998). Lykens and Eysenck showed that psychopaths are deficient in the conditioning of anxiety.

3. More General Emotional Deficits

Psychopaths show less significant physiological reactivity to distress cues than did psychopaths, confirming the idea that they are low on empathy (Blair *et al.*, 1997).

4. Early Parental Loss, Parental Rejection and Inconsistency

The most popular generalization about the development of psychopaths and anti-social personality is the assumption of some form of early disturbance in family relationships.

5. A Developmental Perspective on Psychopaths (Anti-social Personality)

It has long been known that these disorders generally begin early in childhood, especially for boys, and the number of anti-social behaviours exhibited in childhood is the single best predictor of who develops an adult diagnosis of psychopathic or anti-social personality (Robins, 1978).

6. Socio-Cultural Factors

As indicated earlier that family factor plays an important role in the formation of psychopathic personalities. An environment characterized by the breakdown of social norms and regulations, disorganization, undesirable peer models and a climate of alienation from and hostility toward the broader society appears to produce a type of psychopathic personality. This personality is manifested by inadequate conscience development, lack of concern for others, and destructive anti-social behaviour.

Treatments and Outcomes in Psychopathic (Anti-Social) Personality

In general traditional psychotherapeutic approaches have not proved effective in altering psychopathic and anti-social personalities. The four systems of treatment which are usually recommended for the antisocial personality disorders are as follows:

1. *Individual Psychotherapy:* It is a special psychological technique in which the person or the "client" has to "talk out' all his/her problems without any reservation. It is a sort of conversational therapy. During free and frank conversation with him/her therapist tries to get at the root of the problem that afflicts the client. Therapist advises positive suggestions or practices aiming at gradually minimizing and finally removing the problem. The effectiveness of this method of treatment depends on the sincere cooperation of the client.
2. *Group Therapy:* It implies treatment in groups. It is arranged in separate wards or units in special hospitals or treatment centers. This therapy proved preferable in dealing with anti-social though it has its own limitations.
3. *Drug Therapy:* It implies treatment by the use of specific drugs. In some cases of severely aggressive anti-social personality disorders some specific tranquillizing (nerve soothing) drugs have proved very effective in controlling the marked outbursts of aggressiveness or destructiveness.
4. *Behaviour Therapy:* It is a modern psychological technique which is used for modifying the behaviour and emotions of an individual by breaking or eradicating his/her undesirable habit patterns. There is an important aspect of this treatment while dealing with anti-social. It is to provide some suitable situation to the curing anti-social that improved behaviour becomes a model for others.

Cognitive-Behaviour Treatment

Cognitive-behaviour therapists have developed multifaceted technique that appear to offer some promise of more effective treatment (Losel, 1998; Rice and Harris, 1997). Common targets of cognitive-behaviour interventions with psychopathic include the following (Losel, 1998).

(i) Improving social skills.
(ii) Increasing self-control.
(iii) Increasing self-critical thinking.
(iv) Anger management.
(v) Improving vocational competencies.
(vi) Interpersonal problem- solving.
(vii) Changing anti-social attitude.
(viii) Reducing contacts with anti-social peers.
(ix) Improving positive interactions with non-anti-social peers
(x) Victim awareness.

On the basis of an extensive review of research findings, Bandura (1969, 1973) has suggested three steps that can be used to modify anti-social behaviour through the application of learning principle:

(i) the withdrawal of reinforcements for disapproved anti-social behaviour, and where appropriate, the use of punishment for such behaviour.
(ii) the modelling of desired behaviour.
(iii) the reduction of material incentives.

Prevention of Psychopathic and Anti-Social Personality Disorders

During the transition to school years, Patterson and his colleagues have developed programmes targeting the family environment which teach effective parental discipline and supervision At-risk children whose families receive such interventions do better academically, are less likely to associate with delinquent peers, and are less likely to get involved in drug use. Such family or parent training can even be effective in reducing and preventing further anti-social behaviour in children and adolescents already engaged in anti-social behaviour, although conducting the intervention with pre-elementary school aged children was more effective.

The most dangerous psychopaths from the standpoint of society as a whole are those who are not only intelligent and completely unscrupulous but also show sufficient self control and purpose fullness of behaviour to achieve high political office.

QUESTIONS

A. Long Answer Type Questions

1. Explain the concept of 'Anti-social personality disorder'. Are they considered neurotic or psychotic? Discuss.
2. Describe characteristics of anti-social personality disorder in detail.
3. Discuss the causes of psychopaths. Are they born or made?
4. Discuss treatment and outcomes of psychopathic personality.
5. Who are psychopaths? What can a teacher do if he finds such an adolescent in the school?

B. Short Answer Type Questions

1. Explain psychotherapeutic approaches.
2. Discuss treatment and outcomes of psychopathic personality.
3. Discuss individual psychotherapy.
4. Explain cognitive behaviour treatment.
5. Prevention of psychopathic personality disorder.

C. Objective Type of Questions

1. The family environment which teach effective parental discipline and supervision programme was developed by;
   (*a*) Patterson (*b*) Watson
   (*c*) Bandura (*d*) B. F. Skinner
2. Psycho-analysts stressed the importance of unconscious motives and repressed mental conflict. True/False
3. Psychopaths generally have no callous disregard for the rights, needs and well being of others. True/False
4. 1. Psychopath has ability to impress and exploit others.
   2. Psychopaths are seldom able to keep close friends.
   (*a*) I is true II is false (*b*) II is true I is false
   (*c*) both are true (*d*) both are false
5. Anti-social personality disorders appear unable to understand and accept ethical values except on a verbal level.

SUGGESTED READINGS

1. Buss, A. H. (1961). *The Psychology of Aggression,* New York, John Wiley.
2. Jourard, S. M. (1964). *The Transparent Self: Self-disorders and Well-Being*. Princeton, N.J.:D. Van Nostrand.
3. Leon, G. R. (1974). *Case Histories of Deviant Behaviour,* Boston, Holbrook Press.

4. Lorenz, K. (1964). *On Aggression*, New York, Bantam Books.
5. Morris, K. Holland, (1981). *Introductory Psychology* D.C. Heath and Company, Toronto.
6. Mussen, P.H. (1970). *et. al., Child Development and Personality* (3rd Ed.), A Harper International edition, Harpers and Row, New York.
7. Sarason, I. G. and Sarason B. R., *Abnormal Psychology*, Prentice-Hall of India Pvt. Ltd., New Delhi (8th Ed.).

16

Internalizing Disorders

Children with anxiety disorders are more extreme in their behaviour than those experiencing 'normal' anxiety. These children appear to share many of the following characteristics:

1. Over sensitivity
2. Unrealistic fear
3. Sleep disturbances
4. Fear of school.

Children diagnosed as suffering from an anxiety disorder typically attempt to cope with their fears by becoming overly dependent on others for support and help. In DSM IV, anxiety disorders of childhood and adolescence are similar to anxiety disorders in adults (Albano, Chorpita and Barlow, 1996).

There are two additional anxiety disorders of children and adolescence:

(i) Separation anxiety disorder.
(ii) Selective mutism anxiety disorder.

(i) Separation Anxiety Disorder

It is the most common of the childhood anxiety disorders (Bernstein and Borchard, 1991). Such children are characterized by unrealistic fears, over sensitivity, self-consciousness, nightmares and chronic anxiety. They lack self-confidence, are apprehensive in new situations, and tend to be immature for their age. Such children are described by their parents as shy, sensitive, nervous, submissive, easily discouraged, worried, and frequently moved to tears. Typically, they are overly dependent, particularly on their parents.

This disorder is excessive anxiety about separation from major attachment figure, such as mother, and from familiar home surroundings.

When children with separation anxiety disorder are actually separated from their attachment figures, they become pre-occupied with morbid fears, such as the worry that their parents are going to become ill or die. Separation anxiety is more common in girls (Majcher and Pollack, 1996), and the disorder is not very stable in children. Some children go on to exhibit school refusal problems (a fear of leaving home and parents to attend school) and continue to have adjustment difficulty over time and make difficult work and life adjustment later.

(ii) Selective Mutism

Another anxiety based disorder sometimes found in childhood is selective mutism; a condition that involves the persistent failure to speak in specific social situations—this disorder should be diagnosed only if the child actually has the ability to speak and knows the language. This disorder to be diagnosed the condition must have lasted for a month and not be limited to the first month of school when many children are shy or inhibited. Mutism is apparent quite rare and most typically seen at pre-school age. The disorder occurs in all social strata. The child showed early signs of the problem such as shyness, and internalizing behaviour (Stein Hanger and Juri, 1996).

Causal Factors in Separation Anxiety Disorder

Both genetic and learning factors have been cited as possible causal factors underlying the disorder. Steinhausen and Adamek (1997) reported some evidence that genetic factors played a part in selective mutism because these cases tended to occur more frequently in families in which taciturn behaviour was prominent.

A number of causal factors have been emphasized in explanation of childhood anxiety disorders. The major important factors appear to be following:

1. Anxious children often manifest an unusual constitutional sensitivity that makes them easily conditionals by aversive stimuli *e.g.* Such children may be readily upset by even small disappointments.
2. The child can become anxious because of early illnesses,

accidents, or losses that involved pain and discomfort. The traumatic nature of certain life changes such as moving away from friends and into new situations can have also an intensely negative effect on a child's adjustment.

3. Over anxious children often have the modelling effect of an over anxious and protective parent who sensitizes a child to the dangers and threats of the outside world. Often the parent's over protectiveness communicates a lack of confidence in the child's ability to cope, thus reinforcing the child's feeling of inadequacy (Dadds, Heard and Rapee, 1991).
4. Indifferent or detached parents also foster anxiety in their children. Although the child is not necessarily rejected, neither is he or she adequately supported in mastering essential competencies and in gaining a positive self-concept. Repeated experiences of failure, stemming from poor learning skills, may lead to subsequent patterns of anxiety or withdrawal in the face of 'threatening' situations. Other children may perform adequately but are over critical of themselves and feel intensely anxious and devalued when they perceive themselves as failing to do well-enough to earn parents' love and respect.

Treatment and Outcomes

Teachers who are aware of the needs of both over anxious and shy, withdrawn children are often able to ensure successful experience for them that help alleviate anxiety. Behaviour therapy procedures sometimes used in school settings, often help anxious children. Such procedures include assertiveness training, to provide help with mastering essential competencies, and desensitization to reduce anxious behaviour.

The treatment intervention involved holding group sessions with the children in whom they were taught to recognize their anxious feelings and deal them more effectively than they otherwise would have.

Overanxious Disorder of Childhood

This disorder of childhood is a form of the generalized anxiety disorder found in adults. The child or adult experiences excessive apprehension about a number of future events or activities. This worry is present most of the time and is accompanied by one of the following:

(i) restlessness,
(ii) excessive fatigue,
(iii) problem in concentration,
(iv) irritability,
(v) muscle tension, and
(vi) disturbed sleep.

Children tend to be perfectionist, overly compliant, and unsure of them. They may be worry about catastrophic events such as an earthquake or flood. They are often concerned about their competence as well they are doing even in situations where others are not evaluating them The following disorders will be discussed here:

(i) Fears and phobias.
(ii) Obsessive-compulsive disorder.
(iii) Depression.

(i) Fears and Phobias

Phobia is a type of irrational fear. Most children's fears disappear as they grow older even without treatment while some children's fears are intense and disturbing and are appropriate objects of professional concern even if they may disappear spontaneously later. Not only may they cause the child great distress, but they may also interfere with social development. To appreciate the impact of a childhood phobia on the child and her family, Assume Rani, age 7, who has an irrational fear of dogs? She will not go out to play even in her own playground because a dog might come near. She is unable to walk to school or go on errands, so she must be required help every where. Such phobias and other fears that continue beyond the age at which they normally would disappear can often be treated effectively using a behavioural approach such as systematic desensitization or modelling. At the beginning of therapy the fearful child observes another child or adult interacting in the feared object gradually until finally he or she interacts with it as the model does. This adaptation of social learning theory, stimulated by the work of Albert Bandura and others.

Modelling of a somewhat different sort, called symbolic modelling, can be used to prepare children for frightening and unfamiliar situations such as hospitalization or dental work. This procedure typically uses a realistic film that shows the child what to expect. Studies have shown that symbolic modelling may be an effective aid in reducing anxiety (Melamed and Bush, 1986).

(ii) Obsessive – Compulsive Disorder

Obsessions involve the persistent intrusion of intense, unwanted, senseless thoughts, while compulsions are marked by repetitive, ritualistic behaviour. Many children engage in mild rituals and obsessions as part of their normal development. Sometimes, certain acts develop into more disruptive obsessive – compulsive behaviours that require treatment. Children affected by obsessive – compulsive disorder are likely to spend much of their day in rituals and obsessive thoughts, which severely restricts their functioning. However such a severe degree of behaviour in childhood is rare. It begins at least by adolescence and continues relatively unchanged into adulthood (Zeitlin, 1986).

Treatment: It may include medicated and a variety of behaviour and cognitive therapies.

(iii) Depression

There is children who often think such thoughts as 'I am dumb, ugly, and stupid', 'I wish I were dead', and 'you do not love me'... Studies confirm that many youngsters often feel sad. DSM- IV does not contain a special diagnostic category or description for depression in childhood; instead, uses the adult criteria with minor modifications. Depressed mood occurs less frequently in young children and becomes more common in adolescence. Although depression may occur much earlier, the peak risk period for depression is mid-and late adolescence (Van Hasselt and Hersen, 1994). Childhood depression includes behaviours such as withdrawal, crying, avoidance of eye contact, physical complaints poor appetite, and even aggressive behaviour and in some cases suicide (Pfeffer, 1996).

Common Signs of Depression in Children and Adolescents

Although these symptoms may be present in either boys or girls, each symptom tends to more common in one sex than in the other.

More Common Signs of Depression in Girls

1. Body image distortion. Feeling 'ugly' or otherwise unattractive.
2. Loss of appetite and weight, eating less and eating erratically.
3. Lack of satisfaction. Being upset about herself, about life at school and at home and about social life.

More Common Signs of Depression in Boys

1. Imitability being easily angered and hostile, snapping at family, friends and teachers.
2. Social withdrawal, ceasing to spend time with friends, spending most of the time alone.
3. Drop in school performance, loss of interest in and enthusiasm about school and other activities.

Childhood depression s difficult to define and study because its characteristics are variable depending upon the age of the child and his or her cognitive and social abilities.

Causal Factors of Depression in Childhood and Adolescents

Biological Factors

There appears to be an association between parental depression and behavioural mood problem in children (Thapar and McGuffin, 1996). Children of parents with major depression were more impaired, received more psychological treatment, and had more psychological diagnosis than children of parents with no psychological disorders (Kramer, Warner *et al.*,1998). Depression 'runs in families' (Hammen, 1992). This indicates that many depressed children have depressed parents.

Environmental Factors

The undesirable family environments and poor relationships with parents, siblings and peers are common in children with mood disorders and parental tension and their divorce bring on symptoms of depression. These symptoms may reflect the child's feelings of hopelessness and helplessness about the situation. Learning maladaptive behaviour appears to be important in childhood depression disorders (Kaslow, Deering and Recusin, 1994). Children who are exposed to negative parental behaviour or negative emotional states may develop depressed affect themselves. Extensive research supports the view that the patterns of mother-infant behaviour are critical to the development of attachment in a child and that depression in the mother can adversely affect the infant (Martinez, Malphurs *et al.*, 1996).

Treatment and Educational Provisions

As we know that depression is difficult to diagnose or to pinpoint because of the importance of its cognitive components. Two psychological approaches, interpersonal therapy and cognitive therapy, have produced promising results when used with depressed adolescents (Mufson, 1993; Mufson *et al.*, 1994).

Interpersonal therapeutic efforts are focused on problems in the child's or teenager's relationships. In this approach the depressed child or adolescent is provided the guidance on how to express feelings more clearly in troubled relationships, as well as assisted in other interpersonal problem-solving skills.

Another promising approach is a cognitive group approach that may be carried out in after-school classes (Clark *et al.*,1993). In these classes children learn that they have some control over their moods and that they can change the way they feel by changing the way they think.

Suicide

Taking one's life is a significant factor in all depressive states.

Who Attempts and Commits Suicide?

Suicide attempts primarily are actions of young people; at least two-third of attempts of suicide attempters are under 35 (Hawton, 1992)

Suicide in Children and Adolescents

The rates of completed suicide among teenagers and even children seem to be increasing at alarming pace (King, 1997; Speier *et al.*, 1995). The trend is by no means limited to youngsters from deprived or troubled backgrounds. Children from all backgrounds and social status are vulnerable (Joffe and Orford, 1990), and suicide rates for children from affluent families are also on the increase. Children are at increased risk for suicide if they have lost a parent or have been abused (Wagnor, 1997). The forms of psychopathology associated with those environmental risk factors are, not surprisingly, also known to be risk factors for suicide in children's depression, anti-social behaviour and impulsivity (Sokol and Pfeffer, 1992).

Known Risk Factors for Adolescent Suicide

Studies attempting to distinguish who is at risk for a completed suicide, as opposed to a nonfatal attempted suicide, find that conduct disorder and substance abuse (especially alcohol) are relatively more common among the nonfatal attempters (Berman and Jobes, 1992). Availability of firearms in the home is also more common in those who complete suicide than in those who attempt it (King, 1997). Many college students seem peculiarly vulnerable to the development of suicidal motivations. The combined stressors of academic demands, social interaction problems, and career choice—perhaps interacting with challenges to their basic values—evidently make it impossible for some students to continue making the adjustments their life situations demand.

Hopelessness

Negative expectations or hopelessness is an important theme for those who have suicidal preoccupations. These individuals may come to believe that suicide is their only possible strategy for dealing with insoluble problems. Researcher found that for drug and alcohol abusers, a group generally at high risk for suicide, those who were not high in hopelessness was at the risk for suicide (Young *et al.*, 1994).

Warning Signs for Student Suicide

A change in a student's mood and behaviour is a significant warning of possible suicide. Characteristically, the student becomes depressed and withdrawn, undergoes a marked decline in self-esteem, and shows deterioration in personal hygiene. Those signs are accompanied by a profound loss of interest in studies often he or she stops attending classes and stays at home most of the day. Usually, the student's distress is communicated to at least one and other person, often in the form of a veiled suicide warning.

In a minority of cases the actual cause of the behaviour is generally considered to be loss of self-esteem and failure to live up to parental expectations rather than academic failure itself. For most suicidal students, both male and female, the major precipitating stressor appears to be either the failure to establish or the loss of, a close interpersonal relationship. Often the break-up of a romance is the key precipitating factor. It has also been noted that significantly more attempts and suicides are made by students from families that have experienced separation, divorce or a death of a parent.

Suicide Prevention and Intervention

Preventing suicide is extremely difficult. One complicated factor is that most people who are depressed and contemplating suicide do not realize that their thinking is restricted and irrational and that they are in need of assistance. The vast majority do not receive the assistance, they desperately need. Most people who attempt suicide do not really want to die and give prior warning of their intentions;

if a person's cry for help can be heard in time, it is often possible to intervene successfully. Another precipitating factor based on the pain and fear and not to experience second time becomes high risk of suicide by those with a mood disorder, it is very important to be able to identify those within the group who are at highest risk so that they can be treated and protected.

Crisis Intervention

The primary objective of crisis intervention is to help a person cope with an immediate life crisis. Adolescent while contemplating suicide is willing to discuss his/her problem with someone who is his friend or senior to him about a suicide. He must be given sincere and reasonable counseling and guidance. It is often possible to avert an actual suicide attempt.

QUESTIONS

A. Long Answer Type Questions

1. Internalized anxiety disorders are more common in children and adolescents. Discuss.
2. Discuss the causal factors in separation anxiety disorder. How can parents and teachers be helpful in overcoming it?
3. Explain overanxious disorder of childhood. How can it be identified?
4. Discuss common type of overanxious disorders of children and adolescents.
5. Discuss the characteristics of depression along with causes and their cures.

B. Short Answer Type Questions

1. How can a depressed child be treated?
2. What relation does exist between environment and depression?
3. Indicate a few common signs of depression in children and adolescents.
4. What is depression?
5. Describe characteristics of Obsessive-compulsive disorder.
6. What is Phobia?
7. Describe causes of suicide in adolescents.

C. Objective Type Questions

1. Obsessions involve the persistent intrusion of intense, unwanted, senseless thoughts. True/False
2. Compulsions are marked by unrepetitive behaviour. True/False
3. Phobia is a type of rational fear. True/False
4. Both genetic and learning factors have been cited causal factors. True/False

5. **Indifferent or detached parents foster anxiety in their children.**
   True/False
6. **Taking one's life is significant factor in all depressive states.**
   True/False

SUGGESTED READINGS

1. Munsinger, Harry (1983). *Principles of Abnormal Psychology*, Macmillan Publishing, New York.
2. Coleman, C. (1976). *Abnormal Psychology and Modern Life*, (5th Ed), D. B. Taraporevala Sons & Co. Pvt. Ltd.
3. Mussen, P.H. and Others (1970). *Child Development and Personality*, (3rd Ed.), A Harper International edition Tokyo.
4. Shanker, Uday, (1997). *Personality Development*, Atma Ram & Sons Delhi.
5. Liebert, R. M. & Others (1979). *Developmental Psychology*, Prentice-Hall of India Pvt. Ltd. New Delhi.
6. Barlow. H. & Durand, V. Mark (1998). *Abnormal Psychology* (2nd Ed.) Brooks/Cole Publishing Company U. S. A.
7. Holland, Morris K. (1981). *Introductory Psychology*, D.C. Heath and Company, Toronto.
8. Sarason and Sarason, B.R. *Abnormal Psychology – The Problem of Maladaptive Behaviour*, Prentice-Hall of India Pvt. Ltd., New Delhi.

17

Eating Disorders

Eating disorders began to increase during the 1950s or early 1960s and have spread rapidly over the ensuing decades. These disorders occur in infancy and childhood. These disorders include pica, in which the child persistently eats non-food substances such as paint, string leaves or pebbles and rumination disorder of infancy, in which the infant regurgitates or spits up partially digested food. However, DSM–IV considers these eating disorders of infancy or childhood to have little in common with the two major eating disorders of most interesting to psychologists:

(i) Anorexia nervosa, and
(ii) Bulimia nervosa.

Both disorders are especially prevalent through adolescence as well as young adulthood, and are more likely to be found in females than in males.

Anorexia Nervosa

The main characteristics is a person's refusal to maintain even a minimally normal body weight. Both the experience and the significance of body-weight and body shape are distorted in those with anorexia. They are likely to compulsively weigh themselves, measure their body parts, and persistently use a mirror to check their bodies. They tend to view weight loss as a sign of unusual self-discipline and weight gain as a sign of failure of self-control. The person eats nothing beyond minimal amounts of food, so that body weight sometimes drops dangerously.

The mean age for onset of anorexia nervosa is 17 years of age, but there seem to be two particularly high risk periods, one at age 14 and other at age 18. The following lists the criteria for anorexia used in DSM–IV.

The researchers have divided anorexics into subgroup *(i)* those who are their primarily because of restricted food intake (the restricted type, and *(ii)* those who, in addition to restricting food intake, use vomiting and purging with laxatives to main low body weight (the binge-eating/purging type).

Overall Criteria

1. Refusal to keep body weight at or above 85 per cent of the generally recognized normal level for age and height.
2. Intense fear of gaining weight or becoming for even when underweight.
3. Disturbance in experience of body weight or shape, undue influence of these factors on self-esteem, or denial of seriousness of health risks of current low body weight.
4. If menstruation has begun, the absence of three consecutive menstrual cycles.

Associative Behaviours

1. Substantial weight loss in a relatively short period.
2. Continued dieting although individual becomes bone-thin.
3. Continual setting of new weight goals after one is reached.
4. Dissatisfaction with appearance claims of feeling fat, even after weight loss goal is reached.
5. Development of unusual interest in food combined with restricted food intake.
6. Development of strange eating rituals *e.g.* Cuts food into tiny pieces or measures every thing before eating extremely small amounts.
7. Secret eating.
8. Obsessiveness about exercising.
9. Appearance of depression much of the time.
10. Binging and purging (for one subgroup)

The primary feature of anorexia nervosa is the obsessive preoccupation with body image and with losing weight. Unlike the true reduction of appetite in depression disorders in anorexia there is a conscious and deliberate refusal of food. Anorexia disturbs the body's functioning in many ways. It may result in such conditions as retarded bone growth, anaemia, dry skin, low body temperature and basal metabolism rate, slow heart rate, and lack of tolerance for cold (Rock and Yager, 1987). If there is vomiting, a number of additional physiological changes are likely to accompany anorexia. One of these, a low level of serum potassium may cause cardiac arrhythmia, a tendency toward changes in heart rate that can result in death.

Causal Factors of Anorexia Nervosa

The causes of anorexia nervosa are unknown. Most clinicians believe that several risk factors play important roles. Prejudices against being fat are strong and stress on thinness is high in many cultural groups. Some career choices link thinness and achievement. These special populations (notably ballet dancers, and fashion models) are especially at risk for the development of anorexia (Goldbloom and Garfinkel, 1990). Another group that seems at risk is elite female athletes, particularly leanness. Higher levels of disordered behaviour were associated with desire to weight loss, lower self-esteem and greater endorsement of socio-cultural values of thinness (Petrie, 1993).

The Binge-Eating/ Purging Disorder

Binge-Eating Disorder (BED), which is proposed as a separate disorder distinct from bulimia nervosa, nonpurging type. Here the individual binges at a level comparable to bulimia nervosa patients but does not regularly engage in any-form of inappropriate 'Compensatory' behaviour to limit weight gain (even exercise). Not surprisingly most such persons are overweight, but that is apparently not a factor distinguishing them from the group of nonpurging bulimia nervosa patients (Walsh and Garner). The binge-eating/ purging and restricting subgroups of anorexia may have different causes. Those who are in this group are more likely than those in the restrictor group to abuse alcohol or drugs and to have other problems of impulses control, such as stealing (Leon and Ohelan,1984). Genetic factors may play a role at least in the binge-eating/ purging subtype of anorexic disorders. Some researchers have concluded that overall anorexia is intergenerationally transmitted because anorexia nervosa is eight times as common in close relatives of those in a control group of patients with other types of problems (Strober *et al.*, 1990). Minuchin (1978) found several common characteristics among families who have a child with anorexia disorder, enmeshment, over protectiveness, rigidity and lack of conflict resolution. The enmeshed family is one in which no one can be individual, have a separate identity and the insistence on togetherness results in the lack of privacy. Tolerance for conflict is also extremely low in these families.

Treatment and Educational Provision

Treatment range from individual approaches (including psychotherapy and anti-depressant medications) to family therapy, assertiveness training and nutritional training. Two major psychologically based therapeutic approaches used in treating anorexia are behavioural methods and family therapy; these techniques are often used together and combined with nutrition management. In behavioural programmes hospital privileges are made dependent on weight gain. While this technique often leads to increase in body weight, it has some negative features. If the weight gain required is too great patients may develop bulimia and use laxatives and vomiting as a method of weight control (Leon and Phelan, 1984).

Some researchers have focused on family therapy especially for younger anorexic individuals. The individual therapy emphasized building ego-strength and autonomy as well as achieving insight into personal, emotional blocks related to eating. The family therapy approach produced a greater weight gain.

Bulimia Nervosa

Bulimia nervosa is an eating disorder in which eating a larger amount of food—typically, more junk food than fruits and vegetables—than most people would eat under similar circumstances (Fairburn and Cooper, 1993).

Overall Criteria

1. Recurring episodes of binge—eating with the following characteristics:
   (a) Eating within a discrete period of time a much larger amount of food than most people would eat similar circumstances and in a similar time period.
   (b) A sense of lack of control or inability to stop eating during a binge episode.
2. Inappropriate compensatory behaviour to prevent weight gain including self-induced vomiting, misuse of laxatives, diuretic, enemas or other medications, excessive exercise, fasting periods.

3. Binges and compensatory behaviour occurring at least twice a week for at least 3 months.
4. Body shape and weight unduly influencing self-view.
5. These behaviours occurring not only during episodes of anorexic nervosa.

Associative Behaviours

- Consumption of large amounts of food without weight gain.
- Drug and alcohol abuse.
- Appearance of depression much of the time.
- Excessive exercise that interferes with important activities.
- Attempts to conceal symptoms.

Possible Causes

Bulimia may be related to a genetic component of mood disorders as is suggested by the higher incidence of both mood disorders and alcoholism in relatives of bulimic individuals. However, psychological factors may also contribute to bulimic behaviour. It seems likely that certain personality factors make some people more vulnerable to family and social experiences that have negative effect on self-esteem and feelings of self-efficacy. Some theorists have suggested that children who have been seriously abused may be more likely to develop eating disorders (Waller, 1994).

Generalized Risk and Causal Factors in Eating Disorders

Self-Ideal Body Image Discordance

There is now a general socio-cultural factor idealizing extremes of thinness in women in 'advanced' cultures (and by cultural diffusion, elsewhere) is beyond question.

One important product to be thin is that girls and women often develop highly intrusive and pervasive perceptual biases regarding how 'fat' they are. Probably the most important of these are the perceptual discrepancies between the image the girls or young women has of her own body and the 'ideal' female form as represented in contemporary media. Such perceptual biases lead girls and women to believe that men prefer more slender shapes than they in fact do.

Biological Considerations

As with many other disorders, the tendency to develop eating problems runs in families and may therefore indicate some hereditary contribution (Strober, 1995; Walters *et al.*, 1992). Garner (1997) also points out the implications of set—point theory, which refers to the well—established tendency for persons' bodies to 'resist" marked variation from some sort of biologically determined individual norm (the 'set point'), at least over limited time periods. Thus any individual intent on achieving and maintaining a significant decrease in body mass below his or her individual set point may face the opposition of innate compensatory homeostatic mechanisms shared by all of us.

Psychopathological Vulnerability

Some people are more susceptible than others to the development of self-defeating reactions to the inevitable challenges of life. The sources of this fragility are undoubtedly partly inherited, but they are also the outcome of experiences of stressors, the methods employed by the individual to address them, and the relative success of those methods in re-establishing a forward developmental cases of eating disorder, suggests that many of the people having them may be generally ill-occupied to deal with life problems in resourceful manner. Psychologists often refer to this generalized vulnerability pattern as one involving high 'neuroticism' in the person's personality make up. Such people may be anxious, angry, hostile, depressed, self-conscious, impulsive and highly vulnerable to stressors (Costa and Widiger, 1994).

Treatment and Educational Provisions of Bulimia Nervosa

Anti-depressant drugs together with a variety of cognitive and behavioural techniques have been used to treat bulimia. The cognitive and behaviourally based treatments focus on breaking the binge—purge cycle either by preventing binges or by preventing purges. The treatments often involve self-monitoring, relaxation training, identifying and modifying cognitive distortions and developing enhanced feelings of self-efficacy and altering the environment as necessary.

In behavioural approach the patients are first instructed to eat a small amount of a food they ordinary binge on in order to trigger the impulse to binge and then to try to resist that urge response prevention.

QUESTIONS

A. Long Answer Type Questions

1. Explain common major eating disorders of adolescence in detail.
2. Explain the term 'Anorexia Nervosa'. How can it be identified among adolescents?
3. Discuss the causal factors of anorexia in detail.
4. Discuss overall symptoms of 'Bulimia Nervosa'. How can it be controlled?
5. How can 'anorexia nervosa' and 'bulimia nervosa' be treated? Discuss.

B. Short Answer Type Questions

1. Discuss treatment and educational provisions of the adolescents who suffer from anorexia nervosa.
2. Discuss symptoms of anorexia nervosa.
3. How can bulimia nervosa be identified?
4. Why do adolescents suffer from anorexia?
5. Discuss possible causes of bulimia nervosa.

C. Objective Type Questions

1. There are two major eating disorders one is__________and another is __________.
2. Adolescents who suffer from anorexia nervosa weigh their body parts and use mirror to check their bodies. True/False
3. Adolescents who suffer from anorexia nervosa continued dieting although they become bone-thin.
4. Adolescents who suffer from anorexia nervosa have intense fear of gaining__________or becoming for even when__________.
5. Binge-Eating Disorder (BED) is proposed as a separate disorder distinct from bulimia nervosa.

SUGGESTED READINGS

1. Munsinger, Harry (1983). *Principles of Abnormal Psychology,* Macmillan Publishing, New York.
2. Coleman, C. (1976). *Abnormal Psychology and Modern Life* (5th Ed), D. B. Taraporevala Sons & Co. Pvt. Ltd.
3. Mussen, P.H. & Others (1970). *Child Development and Personality* (3rd Ed.), A Harper International edition Tokyo.
4. Barlow, H. & Durand, V. Mark., (1998). *Abnormal Psychology* (2nd Ed.), Brooks/Cole Publishing Company U. S. A.
5. Holland, Morris K. (1981). *Introductory Psychology* D.C. Heath and Company, Toronto.
6. Sarason, & Sarason, B. R. (2000). *Abnormal Psychology – The Problem of Maladaptive Behaviour,* Prentice-Hall of India Pvt. Ltd., New Delhi.

18

Behavioural Problems

AGGRESSION

The term aggression refers to fighting or attacking behaviour. It is a form of interaction, since it occurs between people, and it has the purpose or intent to hurt and injury. Anger is the feeling or emotion that accompanies aggression. The most common form of aggression is:

(i) Instrumental aggression which is intended to gain an object or privilege or strong action aimed at claiming an object, place or privilege—not intended to harm, but may lead to harm.

(ii) *Hostile Aggression*: Bold and direct action that is intended to hurt someone else *i.e.*, unprovoked attack.

(iii) *Overt Aggression*: A form of hostile aggression that involves physical attack.

(iv) *Relational Aggression*: A form of hostile aggression that involves verbal attacks and other actions meant to harm social relationships. Insult, gossip, exclusion, taunts—all these forms of relational aggression, sometimes called social aggression as the intent is to harm social connections. Some children show abnormally high rates of hostility, they verbally and physically assault others with little or no provocation. If they are allowed to continue, their belligerent behaviour can lead lasting delays in moral development and deficits in self-control, resulting in anti-social life style.

Theories of Aggression

The Instinct Theory of Aggression

The instinct theory of aggression proposes that individuals have innate aggressive tendencies. It is argued that aggression is universally present human and animal life and that there is a distinct biological basis for aggression in certain brain structures. Although we all have innate biological structures that make us aggressive but do not determine the direction or the form of the aggressive acts. It is the learning that involved the type of aggressive actions. Freud viewed aggression as one of two basic instincts. The energy of the death instinct builds up within the organism until it must be discharged, either outwardly through overt aggression or inwardly in the form of self-destructive acts. The best that society could do would be to modify its intensity by promoting positive emotional attachments between people and by providing substitute outlets.

The Reaction Theory of Aggression

According to this theory, aggression occurs in response to external stimulation; it is a reaction to, and a way of coping with, events in the environment. Attack is often followed by counterattack, in both animals and humans. If some one hit you, you might hit back. Several studies have shown that aggression seems to be an automatic reaction to pain, so long as there is something nearby to attack.

The Frustration—Aggression Hypothesis

Theorists in the Freudian tradition rejected the idea that aggression was an innate drive or instinct and proposed that it was a frustration-produced drive. Aggressive human behaviour occurs in certain specific situations and not in others. What situations might lead to aggression is the frustration-aggression hypothesis. It states that aggression is always a consequence of frustration, that is, the stimulus for aggressive responses is frustration. The expression of aggression reduces the drive. Aggression is the dominant response to frustration. By this formulation aggression is not inborn, but since frustration is a fairly universal condition, it is still a drive that must find an outlet. Studies have made it clear that aggression often follows frustration, but this is not always the case. This hypothesis works for those cases only if 'frustration' is defined as any event that precedes aggression and 'aggression' is defined to include unobservable internal processes. In this way, whenever a clearly frustrating event is observed that is not followed by an observable aggressive response, it is possible to claim that there was an aggressive reaction but it internal and therefore not observable.

The Social-Learning Theory of Aggression

This theory rejects the notion of aggression as an instinct or frustration–produced drive and proposes that aggression is no different from any other learned response. It can be learned through observation or imitation, and the more often it is reinforced the more likely it is to occur. Aggression results from imitation and reinforcement. In social-learning view, the emotional arousal caused by unpleasant experiences can lead to any number of different behaviour depending upon the behaviour that has been rewarded or has proved successful in the past. Cognitive factors including knowledge of the results of past behaviour and appraisal of positive and negative incentives operating in the current situation enable the individual to anticipate the consequences of behaviour and act accordingly (Modified after Bandura, 1973).A number of studies, according to Bandura (1973) show that aggressive responses can be learned by being reinforced or through imitation.

(a) *Imitating Models:* Children learn through imitating adults. The adults serve as models for the children to copy, whether the adults appear in 'real life' or in film or television. Children exposed to aggressive adult models will themselves act more aggressively. Children imitate their parents, and parents are often aggressive. They aggress against children when they use physical punishment. The best predictor of aggressiveness in children is aggressiveness in their parents.

(b) *Reinforcement:* Children learn that aggression "pays", it is often rewarded or reinforced. We not only learn aggression by observing and imitating others but we also learn it because it has rewarding consequences. Reinforcement for aggression is provided both by parents and the peers.

(c) *Emotional Arousal:* Many parents feel that their children are more likely to become aggressive when they are upset, agitated or excited. Research has shown that emotional arousal does appear to influence a child's willingness to aggress and that the process may operate differently according to the youngster's sex. Boys' overall level of aggression increases when they are emotionally aroused, whereas arousal has been found to decrease aggressive behaviour in girls (Harris & Siebel, 1976).

(d) *Frustration:* One view of how aggression is elicited is found in the famous." Frustration—aggression" hypothesis, it was first spelled out by John Dollard and his associates at Yale in 1939. These theorists argued that frustration, defined as any kind of blocking of goal—directed activity, naturally leads to aggression and aggression was said to be always a consequence of frustration and frustration was said to lead always to some form of aggression.

The Family as Training Ground for Aggressive Behaviour

The child-rearing practices that undermine moral internalization and self-control are related to aggression. Love, withdrawal, power, assertion, physical punishment and inconsistent discipline are linked to anti-social behaviour from early childhood through adolescence in children of both sexes (Coie and Dodge, 1998). Home observations of aggressive children reveal that anger and punitiveness quickly create a conflict-ridden family atmosphere and an 'out of control' child. Children's tendency to engage in destructive, injurious behaviour increases under certain environmental conditions. When the peer group atmosphere is tense and competitive, hostility is more likely (Derosier *et al.*, 1994). These group characteristics are more common in poverty—stricken neighbourhood with a wider range of stressors, including poor-quality schools, limited recreational and employment opportunities and adult criminal subcultures (Pagam *et al.*, 1999).

There is a general agreement among investigators that the family setting of the unsocialized aggressive child is typically characterized by rejection, harsh and inconsistent discipline, and general frustration. Frequently the parents are unstable in their marital relationships, are emotionally disturbed and provide the child with little in the way of consistent guidance, acceptance or affection.

Treatment and Educational Provisions

The treatment of aggressive child is likely to be ineffective unless some means can be found for modifying the child's life setting. This is difficult where the parents are maladjusted and in conflict between themselves.

The advent of behaviour therapy techniques has, however, made the outlook much brighter for children manifesting aggressive reactions. The most important is training of the parents in control techniques, so that they function as therapists in reinforcing desirable behaviour and modifying environmental conditions that may be reinforcing the maladaptive behaviour.

Helping Children and Parents Control Aggression

Help for aggressive children must break the cycle of hostilities between family members and promote effective ways of relating to others. Interventions with pre-school and school age children have been most successful. Once anti-social patterns persist into adolescence, so many factors act to sustain them that treatment is far more difficult.

Coaching, Modelling and Reinforcing Alternative Behaviours

Procedure based on social learning theory has been devised to interrupt destructive family interaction. Several parent—training programmes have been developed in which a therapist observes inept practices, models, alternatives and parents have to practice them (McMahon, 1999). Parents learn not to give in to an acting-out child and not to escalate forceful attempts to control misbehaviour. In addition they are taught to pair commands with reasons and to replace verbal insults and spanking with more effective punishments, such as time out, and withdrawal of privileges.

Social-Cognitive Interventions

Social-cognitive treatments focus on improving social information processing in anti-social youths. Adolescents are taught to attend to relevant no hostile social cues; seeking additional information before acting and evaluate potential responses in terms of their effectiveness. The intervention led to increased skill in solving social problems, decreased endorsement of beliefs supporting aggression, and reduced hostile impulsive behaviours (Guerra and Slaby, 1990).

TEMPER TANTRUMS

Temper tantrum is related to the important emotion, known as anger which has strong impact on the development of child's personality. In the fit of anger the child feels perplexed jealousy and the feeling of revenge. He tries to harm the person or him/her of his /her anger. Every parent experienced that the child immediately gives out his/her reactions whenever feels angry. It is well-known fact that anger is an intense emotion which often results undesirable behaviour. In case of children, such reactions are expected to occur more among them as they have not yet developed appropriate and proper self-control and to postpone their gratification of immediate needs. At this juncture whenever parent prevents such an any desire, or an act of child, anger automatically is stimulated in the child. It is the responsibility of the parents to make them learn to control his/her anger. This controlled learning would definitely help to develop good habits and emotionally balanced and mature personality. We may define a temper tantrum as an uncontrolled outburst of anger expressed through such apparently unserviceable acts as those of screaming, kicking, or holding the breath, and even rolling on the ground may have proved themselves to the most effective means for getting one's own way." It is a physical demonstration of a child's resentment and frustration; the behavioural expressions are shyness sullenness and moodiness.

The temper tantrum is more common among children of pre-school age, especially between 2-4 years. It is the period when the child's emotional needs are very strong. He/she wants to do every thing himself/herself such as dress, feed, and go out on his/her own. But this natural desire of a child to grow is often discouraged by his/her parents as they cannot afford to spend time and wait until the child finishes doing a job in hand quickly or hurriedly run to the child for offering help which the child does not like, he feels frustrated and it led to anger. This is one of the reasons of outbursts of temper.

Boys' and girls' manifestation of anger consisted of tantrum and other undirected outbursts of motor activity. Peevishness, whining and sulking became more commons.

Expressions of anger as children grew older and display of simple undirected energy decreased in frequency. With advancing age the forms of behaviour displayed during anger become more definitely directed toward a given end, while primitive bodily responses of the infant and young child are gradually replaced by substitute reactions commonly of a somewhat less violent and more symbolic in character.

Causes of Temper Tantrums

Followings are the major causes of temper tantrums:

(i) *Physiological Disorders:* Physical conditions of the child is one of the reasons of his temper tantrums such as poor and defective eating habits lack of sleep, rest or lack and poor bladder or bowel clearing. Organic defects like epilepsy, head injury, accident, or convalescence after an acute illness may also lead to temper tantrums.

(ii) *Over Protection:* Children get angry when their desires are not fulfilled or their desires are extremely fulfilled. In other words, it may be stated that a child who is full of energy feels restless, irritable, fussy, and angry when he or she is deprived of or restricted to avail opportunities which are indispensable for the normal development of the child. An over-protected and over-sheltered child becomes accustomed to get at his/her sweet will whatever he/she wants. Consequently he/she learns that his/her temper tantrums are a rewarding means of dominating and commanding over his/her surroundings and also of making his/her parents submit to his/her demands. Over-protecting parents are responsible to develop the motive of dependency, it is a wish to be nurtured, aided, comforted, and protected by the parents.

(iii) *Indulgence:* Parents' indulgence (babying, protecting) appears to foster the development of the opposite kinds of personality characteristics. Children from these homes were relatively inactive, unaggressive, lacking in originality and of inferior social status. However such children become accustomed to satisfy their needs with the help of their parents. In addition, indulged children were apprehensive of physical activity and lacked skill in muscular activities. If they are asked to do any activity, they resent it and express temper tantrums.

(iv) *Modelling:* Children are very quick to imitate the behaviour of their parents. They imitate their parents' irritability and temperament especially their tendency of temper tantrum. Some of the family members feel proud from such activities consequently he/she feels to live up to his/her parents' expectations and reflection of their behaviour.

(v) *Emotional Insecurity:* A child who feels unloved, neglected and rejected either in reality or in phantasy, he/she expresses unconsciously temper tantrums to test out reality. This emotional insecurity may develop a fear and this fear reigns at the unconscious level of his/her mind.

How to Manage Temper Tantrums

If the anger of the child is redirected from the very beginning, control over the anger is possible. We can save the child from the development of temper tantrums.

(i) Physical Check-up

Most important step to manage temper tantrums is to have thorough physical examination in order to remove organic disorder in the child. It is essential to check-up general health of the child if there are any problems; all have to be corrected first.

(ii) Modification in Child Rearing Practices

It is very important to find out basically the real cause of temper tantrums. Poor and faulty attitudes of parents are responsible for this problem. In attempting to control and socialize their children's anger, parents used a great variety of techniques, ignoring, spanking, or slapping, removing the source of trouble, diversion of attention and coaxing were used most frequently by parent of children under 2, while scolding, threatening and isolation were most typically used with their children. The method which appeared to be most useful in bringing the outburst to an end often included removal of interferences with motivated activities such as –

- *(i)* granting the child's desire,
- *(ii)* removing the source of trouble,
- *(iii)* diverting the child's attention,
- *(iv)* providing a substitute activity,
- *(v)* ignoring the outburst, and
- *(vi)* imposing isolation.

Coaxing, soothing, reasoning and scolding were effective only if employed in conjunction with other methods. Parents should provide congenial environment for better adjustment of the child in the family. The parents must be strongly assured that their child is not a victim of any mental problem. Proper material to play age mates, sufficient space play important role in the harmonious growth and development of child's personality.

(iii) Emotional Maturity of Parents

Parents should try to avoid the child to be scolded during a temper tantrum; they themselves should control their own temper tantrums. The child must be given proper and satisfactory reasons by the parents to justify why his/her demands are not being fulfilled at this moment. Children should be handled psychologically, although it would take time, but parents should never mind it is to be executed without fail for the proper development of child. Unreasonableness of child's demands must be made clear. All efforts should be made to convince him or her fully. In spite of that if the child still continues his/her tantrums, it should be ignored parents should wait till the storm is over. But the period of indifference should be interfered with attempts of reasoning with child. Otherwise child may interpret wrongly the difference as rejection of his/her annoyed parents. The child who is suffering from temper tantrums must learn that this strategy of 'exploiting' their parents does not pay a dividend and they can dominate the environment by their tantrums. Parents should keep in mind a few certain possible ideas to control temper tantrums:

(i) The child should not be kept under a very strict discipline.
(ii) Parents should not put up too much burden of work in a mechanical manner.
(iii) Parents should also discuss and convince the child that his/her behaviour is not upto the mark according to social norm.
(iv) Parents should encourage to their children when they feel frustrated and become unsuccessful.
(v) Parents should never fulfil unjustified desires of their wards.

LYING

The meaning of lying in the dictionary is telling an untruth *i.e.* fact that is narrated falsely. Lying is a deliberate attempted of wilfully telling, falsifying, distorting and misrepresenting a fact. It also refers to a conscious and total denial of occurrence of some fact. Such children/persons who habitually tell a lie are called liars. But especially the children who are small may say many things that are not correct. They say incorrect things because:

1. they do not have sufficient, adequate and correct knowledge things or situations described or narrated by them.
2. they have wild fantasies in abundance, consequently while presenting the correct picture of an object or an event; it usually gets by the children with their wild fantasies and wishful thinking.

Kinds of Lying

Cyril Burt, a famous British criminologist classified lying into the following eight types:

(i) Playful Lies: Children often tell such lies for the sake of some enjoyment or fun during their infancy or early childhood. Such children can neither be called liars nor it would be regarded any type of crime. Rather such innocent lies at times provide a lot of fun to the elders around

(ii) Fantasy Lies: Such lies express wishful thinking of the children. Fantasy lies tend to become more frequent up to the age of four. They live in a world of colourful fantasy. Description of such lies is the products of their fantasy as if they exist in reality.

(iii) Confusing Lies: When the child fails to distinguish between the correctness and incorrectness of an object or an event. In such circumstances the child tells lies only because of confusion. It is not the fault of the child.

(iv) Vanity-arousing Lies: Vanity of human wishes does not lie only in adults but it has also been observed among in many children. Such children are found to lie just because they enjoy a feeling of false vanity. Such lies provide them with ego satisfaction. Children describe certain things of which they are totally ignorant, and never seen or done the thing at all. Parents and teachers should know that such lies are common among those children who suffer from inferiority complex.

(v) Revengeful Lies: Some of the children who are frustrated from their classmates and are unable to take revenge. Such children go on building false stories about those children who might have defeated them in some competitive situation. It is very clear that spreading of such cooked up lies indicates an unhealthy attempt of the liar to prove his/her superiority over his/her opponent.

(vi) Selfish Lies: Sometimes it happens that a child deliberately tells a lie just in order to conceal some fault in his/her own doings. Such children indulge in such selfish lies as a tool of self-defence mechanism against being exposed to others.

(vii) Lies of Loyalty: A child/person may be loyal to his/her group especially during childhood and adolescence; it

does not matter whether the group is involved in good acts or some other undesirable ones. It has been observed that such a child/person who identifies himself with his group tries to defend or to protect the objectionable activities of the group.

(viii) *Pathological Lies:* There are some children/adolescents who have been observed that they suffer from some special complexes, disorders or abnormalities. Such complexes are often unconsciously reflected in their habit of lying. "A pathological liar is one who indulges in lying for nothing or only for the sake of gratifying himself/herself in an attempt to prove his/her supremacy over others."

Treatment and Educational Provisions

Childhood lying can well be eradicated very easily. But if proper attention has not been paid by the parents and the teachers it would be very difficult to save our children from becoming selfish or habitual liars. Parents' repeated advices and sermons do not yield practically effective results. So many Don'ts' actually spoil the child instead of eradicating lying. Moreover parents should try to find out the root cause of the problem so that proper treatment and effective educational environment may be provided to such children. Parents and teachers may manage the problem of lying as discussed below:

(a) Probe into the Root Cause of Lying

It is very important to find out the root cause or causes, of which lying is just a manifest symptom. This type of searching or in depth exploration of the root cause is to be done specifically and carefully. After the exploration of root cause of lying, the teacher, parents, or clinical psychologist should deconditioned the cause of the child so that he may give up the habit of lying.

(b) Avoidance of Provocative Situations

Parents or teachers should always try to avoid all such situations where a child is likely to be provoked or tempted to lying. The child should only be allowed to play or accompany with those children who have good habits and cultured background. It is also to some extent is fact that child picks up bad habits easily than good ones. Parents and teachers should encourage their children to avoid all such alluring or provocative situations where children are likely to be the victims of lying.

(c) Confession by the Liar

Parents, whenever think that their child is telling a lie, he should immediately to make him realize that he has done something wrong. This confession would create a feeling of repentance, shame, and embarrassment. All such unpleasant feelings will discourage the child for repeating lies in future.

(d) Positive and Effective Instructions

Positive instructions are found most effective means of correcting and curing a child of his lies. Parents and teachers are advised to avoid instructions such as, 'Don't do it', 'don't do it'. As earlier mentioned that so many such remarks spoil the child instead he may be confused and think in his mind "what to do'? The child should be given positive instructions such as 'Do it'. Parents or teachers should encourage the child to speak the truth instead of discouraging a child to tell lies. Every child passes through a phase of negativism. This means a child at a certain stage of development just does the opposite of what he/she is asked not to do. The children actually get satisfaction by negating or defying the instruction of the elders. At this juncture parents should get advantage from this natural tendency.

(e) Punishment

Although it is improper to punish any child for his wrong deed. But it is essential to give psychological punishment to such a child. Psychological punishment includes—stop talking with the child, ignore the child, and showing lack of concern for the child have proved very effective in curing a child of lies. But it must be kept in mind that such treatment should never be continued to a longer period because that may have adverse effect on the development of child's personality. If a child feels rejected for a long period of time, he may get involved in more serious offences. Researchers found that strong feeling of rejection may prompt a child to be aggressive. The main objective of the punishment is to make the child realize that lying is an unhealthy practice.

(f) Fulfillment of the Child's Needs

Every child has basic needs which are to be fulfilled at the stage of development. These needs may either be biological or psychological but their non-fulfillment may lead a child to behave negatively.

Delinquent activities, truancy, offensive behaviour, and telling lies are such activities which are committed by the children. Most of the biological needs are fulfilled in every civilized society. Children, who are in the habit of telling lies, generally suffer from non-fulfillment of psychological needs. Parents and teachers are advised to behave with children in such a manner that their psychological needs be fulfilled as much as possible

QUESTIONS

A. Long Answer Type Questions

1. Explain the term 'aggression'. Discuss its various theories.
2. "Frustration leads aggression". Discuss. How can parents help children to control their aggression?
3. Explain the term 'temper tantrums'. Discuss its various causes.
4. "Temper-tantrums" is the result of frustration. Discuss. How can parents manage it?
5. Explain the term "Lying" Discuss its various kinds. How can parents treat lies of their children?

B. Short Answer Type Questions

1. Discuss social-learning theory of aggression.
2. The family is a training ground for aggressive behaviour. Discuss.
3. "Frustration leads aggression." Discuss.
4. Treatment and educational provisions of children's lies.
5. Elaborate kinds of lying.
6. Discuss the role of emotional maturity in the management of children's temper tantrum.
7. How can parents modify their children's rearing practices to eradicate temper tantrums?

C. Objective Type Questions

1. Aggression refers to fighting or attacking behaviour. True/False
2. The frustration-aggression hypothesis rejects the idea that aggression is an innate drive or instinct. True/False
3. The social- learning theory of aggression was modified by

   (a) Freud *(b)* Adler
   (c) Fromm *(d)* Bandura

4. Frustration-aggression hypothesis was first spelled out by

   (a) John Dollard *(b)* Freud
   (c) Bandura *(d)* Jung

5. Children get angry when their desires are__________fulfilled .

SUGGESTED READINGS

1. Munsinger, Harry, (1983). *Principles of Abnormal Psychology,* Macmillan Publishing, New York.
2. Coleman, C. (1976). *Abnormal Psychology and Modern Life* (5th Ed.), D. B. Taraporevala Sons & Co. Pvt. Ltd.
3. Mussen, P.H. & Others (1970). *Child Development and Personality* (3rd Ed.), A Harper International edition, Tokyo.
4. Shanker, Uday, (1997). *Personality Development,* Atma Ram & Sons Delhi.
5. Liebert, R.M. & Others (1979). *Developmental Psychology,* Prentice-Hall of India Pvt. Ltd., New Delhi.
6. Barlow, H. & Durand, V. Mark (1998). *Abnormal Psychology* (2nd Ed.) Brooks/Cole Publishing Company U.S.A.
7. Holland, Morris K. (1981). *Introductory Psychology,* D.C. Heath and Company, Toronto.
8. Sarason & Sarason, B.R., *Abnormal Psychology – The Problem of Maladaptive Behaviour,* Prentice-Hall of India Pvt. Ltd., New Delhi.

19

Special and Integrated Education

There was a time when people with handicaps and disabilities were treated poorly by other members of society, and children were excluded from school solely on the basis of handicapping conditions. Today, education is a guaranteed right for students with handicaps and disabilities. Despite legal guarantees of right that have belonged for some time to people without disabilities, although life is still not rosy for many people with disabilities as they compare their education with that of siblings or neighbours who were not disabled and speak only of the gaps. Today's adults with disabilities who recall segregated facilities, separate classes, or home instructions can not say enough how inadequate was their academic training. Lipsky and Gartner (1987) suggested that 'the establishment of a separate system of education for the disabled is an outgrowth of attitudes toward disabled people.'

Teachers who refer students for special education, their primary goals are placement programme outside the regular classroom. These teachers believe that an alteration in instructional placement will be a sufficient basis for improving the educational opportunities of the student with special learning needs. Regular education teachers come to believe that there are others in the system that are better able to teach students with academic or learning problems. They assume that students should be sent to places where they can benefit from the services of these people. Undoubtedly some students do require specialized instructions to meet their special learning needs.

As attitudes toward people with disabilities improved and concern for their care became more a social issue, perspective changed from protecting members of society to protect people with disabilities from society. Practices akin to sheltering, nurturing and shielding are the part to provide insulation from the ills of society. Special classes with related special curricula and specially trained teachers are the hallmarks of today's phase. Recently special education entered a period when custodial care and service are viewed either as separate and independent activities or as related aspects of treatment in special education.

Concept of normalization (life as much like other people as possible), mainstreaming (Education as much like other people as possible), least restrictive environment (service in places as much like those provided for other people) and integration (life experiences in regular environments) whenever possible have greatly influenced what is and should be taught in special education programme. Every one is not satisfied with the existence and perpetuation of separate and sometimes unequal special education programmes and facilities. Educators are challenged to work together in identifying and implementing alternatives for meeting the special learning needs of children and youths in regular classrooms (Wang, 1989).

The Concept of Special Education

The term 'special education' refers all aspects of education which helps in developing the personality of exceptional children harmoniously. However, teachers of exceptional children do not usually use the methods of teaching-learning process which are used to teach normal children. Special education segregates to those children who need special attention and education to bring them to mainstream by providing them extra opportunities. Special education is at a crossroads in its development. Early concern for access to free appropriate has been replaced by radical and mature perspectives that put people with special learning needs in regular classes to be educated with every body else. It must be understood first that to what extent special education is a component of regular education or a separate education system. Current organizational practices promote the separation of regular and special education students and programmes.

Kirk (1962) is of the view that the term special education has been used to signify those aspects of education that are applied to handicapped and gifted, but not applicable to average children. It is also true that exceptional children can not be benefited by normal methods of teaching in regular schools. Special education is a means of providing relief for regular classroom teachers and students; it is a reprieve from the rigours of working and learning with students who are difficult to teach.

Special education exists to provide educational opportunities to people with special learning needs.

Needs of Exceptional Learners/Children

AND

Need and Objectives of Special Education for Exceptional Learners/ Children (See Chapter 1)

Learning Aspects of Special Education

We know that only good and effective teaching matters for not only to average children but also to exceptional learners The main difference between teachers of these two types learners is that the teachers of exceptional learners have to worry more about the basic ingredients of good teaching which are specially considered as

1. Curriculum.
2. Expectations or conditions.
3. Outcomes or consequences.

1. Curriculum

The curriculum in special education is based on educational principle. It centered on *(a)* physical (motor and sensory), *(b)* intellectual (speech and academic), and *(c)* moral (socialization) training. The curriculum for exceptional learners involves 'thinking small',' thinking basic', and 'thinking sequentially'.

Every exceptional learner needs help in establishing himself before he seeks admission in regular school and classroom. Teacher must understand all these facts before. The children with handicaps and disabilities ought to be allowed to live as normal a life as possible (*i.e.* normalization) and the implementation of this principle in schools through education of students with handicaps in regular environments.

The possibilities of changed and varying educational curriculum for handicaps are endless. However variation in curriculum may not be so important in educating exceptional children than variation in the environment or circumstances under which they seek academic learning.

2. *Expectations or Conditions*

Certain conditions or expectations must be met before the child is asked to learn the educational task successfully. Every task of learning requires certain level of growth, maturity and development and the teacher or resource teacher must select a proper time to assign the task:

The following conditions must be kept in mind while introducing the task of learning by the teacher.

When: The parents and teacher must choose the proper time to assign the task.

How: Keeping in view the impairment of the student, the teacher should properly instruct the way the task is to be completed.

How Much: Impaired children are to be provided the proper conditions associated with the task to get it done successfully.

How Long: Impaired children will be expected to complete the task successfully within certain time limits.

How Well: Every impaired child will be expected to achieve a certain level of correctness in view of his/her impairment.

The school should provide all the facilities related to learning as it is filled with expectations that must be met if the impaired child is to be considered successful. Resource teacher or regular teacher has constantly to exhibit flexibility in establishing conditions. However time has changed the regular teachers' working with exceptional learners who must be prepared to adjust classroom conditions to meet the needs of impaired children. It is known fact that the selection of curricular tasks and the conditions of learning are totally controlled by the teacher.

3. *Outcomes or Consequences*

The outcomes in learning are important to consider with respect to good teaching. Once the child completes a task, something usually happens. The task itself has been rewarding because of the child's interest or sense of accomplishment. But it may also be unpleasant and frustrating if its level of difficulty is high.

Limited attention has been paid to the special learning and adjustment needs of students with disabilities as educational goals were developed and outcome indicators identified in the late 1980s and early 1990s. There has been some attention to the importance of documenting the outcomes of special education and it can be held account for outcomes. Attention to the issue of special education outcomes and their indicators has taken different approaches. Outcome indicators applicable only to special education are being identified. One approach to identify some common core outcomes to be achieved by all students. It is assumed outcome measures for special should be essentially the same as for general education. There+ may be following over-all groups of outcomes:

1. Attitude and attributes.
2. Skills and competencies.

These have been organized into four categories for special education:

(a) Students participation.
(b) Academic competencies.
(c) Attitude and attributes.
(d) Independent living skills.

Special Education Outcomes

Outcomes -Based Education

It reflects the belief that desired educational outcomes should direct the content of education. The basic notion is that curriculum development should be based on identified outcomes rather than on a listing of subject matter to be covered. Thus specific outcomes are identified as the basis for curriculum development. Spady identified two features of outcomes-based education:

1. *Clarity of Focus:* The instructional organization, components and practices of schools should be designed around the clearly defined outcomes of all students must demonstrate and
2. *Expanded Opportunity:* School must deliberately provide all students with the time and instruction they need to reach essential outcomes goals.

Four outcomes underlying outcomes-based education identified as critical:

1. All students can learn and have success, success breeds success and schools control the conditions for success.
2. Content is prescribed in terms of learner outcomes (what is to be learned) rather than in terms of course syllabus (what is to be taught).

3. Criterion-referenced assessment procedures are specifically developed to measure students' progress on the predetermined outcomes.
4. Instructional design is based on a model in which learning is the constant and time the variable, rather than time being the constant and learning the variable.

Students in special education should fit right in with general education as long as the stated outcomes are appropriate.

Orientation Training

An outcome of multi-sensory experience is orientation, that is, the awareness an individual has about the environment and his or her position in it. Although it is used primarily to describe an important aspect of mobility for the visually handicapped, the broader concept of orientation has relevance for many exceptional learners. Curriculum for such learners must be flexible which means to help exceptional children for their improvement. Frank M. Hewett in his book *Education of Exceptional Learners* has discussed twelve curricular considerations reflecting much of what is inherent in the principle, tasks and activities.

1. *Expect the Child to Learn:* Each exceptional child is to be allowed to understand that the dignity of being expected to learn. There is nothing more degrading or destructive than withholding such dignity or replacing it with pity or neglect.
2. *Take Nothing for Granted*: Be sure that the child is ready for the level of the assigned task.
3. *Bombard the Senses:* The world impinges on us through our senses. Some exceptional children may need to develop intact senses to compensate for deficits in or the lack of one sense but most can see and hear and touch. Combine these senses to involve the child more completely.
4. *Load up the Cues:* Have the child label and describe what is happening, use a variety of distinctive elements.
5. *Make Content Vivid:* Increase the intensity of what is given to the child.
6. *Repeat as Often as Necessary.*
7. *Make the Content Relevant:* Give children content that is familiar and part of their out-of-school lives.
8. *Make it Concrete:* Learning by doing.
9. *Surprise the Child:* Do the unexpected.

10. *Accentuate the Positive:* Make a big deal about what was right, not wrong. When possible ignore mistakes. When it is not possible help the child to understand that if we did not make mistakes we would not know what we had to learn.
11. *Move Sequentially.*
12. *Be Prepared to Back up.*

It is important to consider tasks and activities for increasing social interaction and improving relationships and communications. Learning to gain approval and avoid disapproval is more complex than learning to acquire knowledge and skill about the environment. There are vast individual differences among those with whom the exceptional learner comes in contact and perceives and interact with others makes the building of social skills most difficult. Kirk (1972) calls attention to the 'intangible' nature of social skill training with exceptional learners and concludes that such training can not be taught like physics. The exceptional learners must understand the legal, moral, social expectations of society to improve his/her social skills. He/she should be very sensitive to the feeling of others. To improve social skills include; (1) Modelling, (2) Role playing, (3) Coaching, (4) Shaping, and (5) Integrated group experiences with non-exceptional children.

A comprehensive social skill programme should be devised on the basis of Social Learning Curriculum (SLC) (Goldstein, 1974). Underlying objective of SLC is to build the child's potential for critical thought and for independent action. The theoretical foundations of the programme are drawn from Gestalt psychology in which problem solving involves three stages *viz.*

1. mass stage,
2. differentiation stage, and
3. stage of integration.

At the *mass stage,* the individual must separate the relevant from the irrelevant aspects of the problem situation.

At the *differentiation stage,* the relevant elements are scrutinized individually and in association with one another.

At the *integration stage,* the information and experience from the differentiation stage are integrated and become available to future problem solving.

Exceptional children should be provided such an environment which may refrain them from reaching to stimuli but can direct their energies toward stimuli that are important to their learning and adjustment and through which they can achieve success.

Following reinforcements should be provided to exceptional learners to motivate them so that we can get positive outcomes from their teaching-learning process:

(a) Joy.
(b) Reinforcement for the acquisition of knowledge.
(c) Knowledge of result.
(d) Social approval.
(e) Multi-sensory stimulation and activity.
(f) Task completion.

Adaptive instructions must be given to the exceptional learners so that they themselves may accommodate according to their capacity and ability in teaching-learning process. It is also the responsibility of the students to cooperate in achieving group educational goals.

Special education as treatment; the practice of special education is a three-stage process: (1) The students who are first declared eligible for special education service, (2) They are taught or treated differently, and (3) Their progress is evaluated.

The term treatment and teaching are used synonymously by many professionals. The treatment of students with special learning needs to serve many purposes. *Remediation and compensation* are two of them.

The term remediation is derived from the word 'remedy' something that 'correct, construct or removes' something that has gone wrong. In special education settings, the medical model obtains, and the focus of treatment is often on remediation. Specific skills are taught in an effort to overcome deficiencies in academic skill development or emphasis may be placed on remedying specific deficits in abilities such as memory or perception.

A second purpose of treatment is compensation. This term has been derived from the word 'compensate' which means 'to make up for' usually compensatory treatment are employed when overcoming a problem seems impossible or when compensating for a condition seems easier than trying to correct. Many special education treatments are compensatory. Compensatory activities are usually most apparent in the treatment of sensory or physical disabilities, but are often used with students with other disabilities and handicaps.

Special education as a prevention; when intervention is designed to prevent a disability from becoming a handicaps or to control problem behaviours that sometimes result in classification of students as handicapped.

However the intention is that students 'stay put' in regular education programs rather than be placed in 'pull out' special education environments, it is evident in efforts to adapt instruction to meet individual learner needs and in efforts to enhance the education of difficult-to-teach students in the mainstream.

The real world of learning and school often involves negative consequences. When we criticize children or disapprove of their behaviour in some way, our intention may be positive. We should save our children from possible effects of the teacher's negative remarks. Besides the ideal of bringing about improved behaviour through negative consequences, we, as a teacher or as a parent, should be very cautious while criticizing or disapproving their attainment in any field of the learning especially of the exceptional children. Teacher, according to Hewett and Forness should take into account the following considerations;

1. It should occur only after the child's behaviour has exceeded limits that have been clearly stated previously.
2. It should occur with emotional control, not as a result of teacher with exasperation.
3. It should be presented to the child as a constructive aid to learning rather than as an arbitrary punishment.
4. It should involve a specific period of time rather than an open ended exclusion.
5. It should place the child in the best available setting where multi-sensory and social stimulation is limited.
6. Once the time-out period has passed the child should immediately return to the class without any lecturing.

Success is a True Reinforcer in Learning (Charles Skinner)

Integrated Education—Its Concept

The National Policy on Education (1986), recommended to provide equal opportunity to all not only for access but also for success. Integrated education is very much important to educate the children with special needs and disabilities with the normal children together so that such children may interact with their peer groups and may be able to develop their personality in the same direction. Equalization of educational opportunity is a fundamental right of exceptional children. It is only possible when exceptional children get an opportunity to get their education in the same class and environment.

The term "integration" signifies the process of interaction of disabled children and children in same educational settings. There are two terms which are used synonymously with integration. These are: (1) Mainstreaming, and (2) Normalization.

Mainstreaming refers integrating handicapped or disabled children into regular classes and helping them through specialized techniques.

Sometimes integration is interchangeably used with normalization. The reason is that the disabled children are treated with normal children in integrated education system.

Moreover, integrated education system is an educational programme in which exceptional children attend classes with normal children on either a part or full time basis. It combines social integration or academic integration or both. According to some educationists' integrated education is the placement of the disabled children in common schools with some specialized educational help and services.

Stephens and Black Hurt's definition reveals the fact that "Mainstreaming is the education of mildly handicapped children in the regular classroom. It is based on the philosophy of equal opportunity that is implemented through individual planning to promote appropriate learning, achievement and social normalization."

Kinds of Integrated Education

There are different types of integrated education available for exceptional children.

Following important types of models are worth noting here.

1. The full time integration in normal schools.
2. *Part time Integration*: Disabled children attend regular classes but some classes are suspended owing to the arrangement of special classes.
3. *Education in a Special Class:* Education of the disabled children is arranged in a special class but they are required to maintain their attendance at normal classes. They have also to engage

themselves in co-curricular activities of the normal school.

4. Integrated education in residential schools with some subjects in neighbouring normal schools.
5. A large number of normal children are placed with the disabled children to ensure academic and non-academic participation among themselves.
6. Education in normal classes with home tuition or home-bound programme is included in integrated education.
7. Short term education in hospitals.

Value or Importance of Integrated Education

There are many educationists who nullify the idea of special education on the ground that it never equalizes educational opportunities rather it creates a feeling of differentiation among children. Special classes create a feeling of inferiority complex among disabled children. Modern psychologists are of the opinion that integrated education should be introduced in our school system to provide equal opportunities for education to all children. Following points may justify their point of view:

1. There is every possibility to develop psychological complexes under special educational settings. Integrated education provides opportunity to develop proper mental growth and harmonious development of the exceptional child.
2. *Development of Social Qualities:* Children get wider set-up and this is conducive for the disabled to learn social values in the company of normal children.
3. Integrated education is less expensive. Special educational set-ups are very costly and expensive as compared to provisions given in integrated education.
4. Integrated education is advantageous too.
5. *Learn to Adjust with Environment:* Natural environment is created for interaction of the handicapped with non-handicapped peers. It gives opportunity to learn to adjust with the environment.
6. *Possibility of Academic Integration:* Teachers have always this idea in their mind that the students learning in the special schools are generally under-achievers, consequently they fail to score well in academic studies. In other way it may be stated that congenial atmosphere and proper curriculum and integrated education brings academic integration.

7. Integrated education is based on principle of equality which is fully maintained.

Difference between Special Education and Integrated Education

It may be described in the following way:

Special Education	*Integrated Education*
1. It is an old notion.	1. It is relatively recent idea.
2. It isolates the exceptional from the normal children.	2. It socialized the disabled with normal children.
3. Special education is a kind of clinical.	3. It is based on the principle of psychology.
4. It is based on the law of discrimination.	4. It is based on the principle of equality.
5. Severely handicapped are benefitted.	5. Mildly disabled are benefitted.
6. It is not considered as an integral part of the total education. Special classes are encouraged.	6. It is a part of total education.
7. It provides vocational training and guidance.	7. It provides general education.
8. It is established out side the ordinary school system.	8. Here disabled receive being special in every aspect normal child.

National Policy on Education (NPE): Recommendations

The Handicapped

The objective should be to integrate the physically and mentally handicapped with the general community as equal partners, to prepare them for normal growth and to enable them to face life with courage and confidence. The following measures will be taken in this regard.

1. Wherever it is feasible, the education of children with motor handicaps and other mild handicaps will be common with that of others.
2. Special schools with hostels will be provided as far as possible at district headquarters, for the severely handicapped children.
3. Adequate arrangements will be made to give vocational training to the disabled.
4. Teachers' training programmes will be reoriented, in

particular for teachers of primary classes, to deal with the special difficulties of the handicapped children.

5. Voluntary effort for the education of the disabled will be encouraged in every possible manner.

National Policy on Education Review Committee (NPERC) Revised (1992)

Complemented the NPE for placing the education of the handicapped in the right perspective. The NPE recognizes the education of the handicapped as an integral part of the education process and as an important element of the handicapped, particularly in regard to involvement of voluntary agencies. The NPE, however, felt that the NPE was inadequate in the following respects:

1. NPE had not stressed the mobilization of the total general education system for the education of the handicapped.
2. Special schools had been treated in isolation from other educational institutions from the point of view of providing the educational supervisory infrastructure, leaving it to the Ministries of the Welfare and HRD to cooperatively develop the same.

We feel that it would not be fair to fault the NPE on these counts. As NPERC itself noted that establishment of special schools at district and sub-district levels; curriculum development apart from provision of infrastructure facilities and specific target setting for universal primary education of the handicapped. The centrally sponsored scheme of Integrated Education for the Disabled Children (IEDC) scheme was started in 1974-75 by the then Ministry of Social Welfare. In 1982-83, the scheme was transferred, to the department of Education. When the scheme was transferred, only 2500 students were covered under the scheme. In 1987 the scheme was thoroughly reviewed and revised in pursuance of NPE. Coverage of the scheme was extended to 6000 schools in 22 states. Special schools cater to the children with grave handicaps, and with vastly different needs. These children required more individualized attention.

The NPERC made very useful recommendations relating to the modalities of implementing programmes for the education of handicapped. It had advocated the use of media in creating awareness about the problem of the handicapped, providing support to every family with a handicapped child through incentives, dialogue and training and adopting flexible approach to the education of physically handicapped. The NPERC examined at length the needs of different categories of the mentally retarded and made specific recommendations. The NPERC had also made important recommendations on the role of training and of technological development in the education of the physically handicapped.

Modern Trends in Special Education

Two trends are apparent in special education today. First, children with disabilities are receiving special education services earlier. This trend reflects the recognition that a child's ability to learn in school depends on skills learned as a toddler, such as communications with others or exploring the environment. Since disabilities can delay the acquisition of these skills, early special education is needed to provide a foundation for future learning. To identify these young children and treat their disabilities, special education is working closely with hospitals, medical personnel, therapists and social workers. Family services are being provided to help parents understand their child's disability and its treatment, and pre-school education is being provided in homes and in pre-school education centers. For many children early educational treatment of handicapping conditions can reduce or eliminate the need for intensive special service later.

The second trend is a change in the public's attitude toward employment of people with handicaps. Today it is recognized that valuable contribution may be made even by people with severe handicaps. Schools are assessing the abilities and talents of students with handicaps and matching them with potential occupations. More instruction in vocational skills is being provided to students with handicaps, and programmes are being offered to assist them in the transition from school community life and work.

Emphasis on serving the needs of exceptional children is likely to continue and the information derived from current research will improve special educational services even more in future.

QUESTIONS

A. Long Answer Type Questions

1. What is "Special Education"? Discuss its importance in educating the handicapped children.

2. What is "Integrated Education"? Discuss its importance in educating the disabled students.
3. Who is handicapped child? How can physically handicapped children be integrated into common schools?
4. Explain the concept of "Special Education." How does it differ from Integrated Education?
5. Discuss the need, objectives and importance of special education.

B. Short Answer Type Questions

1. Mainstreaming.
2. Normalization.
3. Modern trends in special education.
4. Special education is important for exceptional learners.
5. Integrated education.
6. Point out the difference between special education and integrated education.
7. Discuss outcomes of special education.
8. Curriculum of special education.

C. Objective Type of Questions

1. Special schools are required to meet the personal and social needs of exceptional learners. True/False
2. Bright children get a chance for proper stimulation in the special class. True/False
3. The special education may be imparted in the regular classroom, special classroom or in combination of both. True/False
4. The term "integration" signifies the process of interaction of disabled children and normal children in the same educational settings. True/False
5. Mainstreaming refers to integrating handicapped or disabled children into regular classes and helping them through specialized techniques. True/False
6. Integration is interchangeably used with normalization. True/False

SUGGESTED READINGS

1. Hewett, F. M. with Forness Steven R. (1984). *Education of Exceptional Learners,* Allyn and Bacon. Inc., London (3rd Ed.)
2. Prasad, J. and Prakash, R. (2003). *Education of Handicapped Children: Problems and Solutions.* New Delhi, Kanishka Publishers & Distributors.
3. Samuel Kirk, A. (1962). *Educating Exceptional Children,* Houghton Mifflin Company, Boston.
4. Shanker, U. (1976). *Exceptional Children,* New Delhi, Sterling Publishers.
5. Sharma, A. (2003). *Fundamentals of Special Education (Integrated Teaching to Mainstreaming),* Surya Publications, Meerut.

6. Teleford, C.W. and Sawrey, J.M. (1967). *The Exceptional Individual,* New Jersey, Prentice Hall Inc.
7. Warnock (1970). *Special Educational Needs*. Report of the Committee of Enquiry into the People, HMSO.

Index